DOODLES ON LEADERSHIP

DOODLES ON LEADERSHIP
EXPERIENCES WITHIN AND BEYOND TATA

R GOPALAKRISHNAN

RUPA

Published by
Rupa Publications India Pvt. Ltd 2019
7/16, Ansari Road, Daryaganj
New Delhi 110002

Sales Centres:
Allahabad Bengaluru Chennai
Hyderabad Jaipur Kathmandu
Kolkata Mumbai

Copyright © R. Gopalakrishnan 2019

The views and opinions expressed in this book are the author's own and the facts are as reported by him which have been verified to the extent possible, and the publishers are not in any way liable for the same.

All rights reserved.
No part of this publication may be reproduced, transmitted, or stored in a retrieval system, in any form or by any means, electronic, mechanical, photocopying, recording or otherwise, without the prior permission of the publisher.

ISBN: 978-93-5333-524-3

Second impression 2020

10 9 8 7 6 5 4 3 2

The moral right of the author has been asserted.

Printed at Parksons Graphics Pvt. Ltd, Mumbai

This book is sold subject to the condition that it shall not, by way of trade or otherwise, be lent, resold, hired out, or otherwise circulated, without the publisher's prior consent, in any form of binding or cover other than that in which it is published.

Contents

Introduction: Balconies of Leadership   *vii*

1. Candid Conversations of Torchbearers and Trailblazers   1
2. Innovation in its DNA   11
3. Tradition of Trusteeship   29
4. Flying Once More Across the Sky   44
5. The #EtTu Movement in India Inc.   72
6. Making 'Little India' Shine   88
7. The Future of Agriculture is not in the Stars   109
8. Navigating the Labyrinth: A Citizen's View of Justice   120
9. Resetting India's Mindsets   141
10. Nation, Society and Business Enterprise   163

Acknowledgements   187
Index   191

Introduction
Balconies of Leadership

During my father's generation, a government job was the most prized. Throughout my career, a corporate job in a well-established and successful organization was highly prized. I wonder what my son's generation will value.

A corporate job can be hugely satisfying. It all depends on how the person lives it. If he or she lives through the job as a means of earning a livelihood, you get one outcome. If the manager lives through it at high levels of engagement and leadership experiences, you get a different outcome. Such an outcome can be hugely satisfying because you first hone your transactional leadership, then develop your corporate leadership capability and finally, try to engage at a holistic level with some—not all—social and societal issues which concern you and/or the corporation.

During the fifty years of my career, I experienced leadership moments and learnings at three levels: transactional, corporate and holistic. I call these the three balconies of experiences and learnings. I should clarify the meaning of each of these three balcony levels as I experienced them.

BALCONY OF TRANSACTIONAL LEADERSHIP

In the first twenty years of my career, largely at Hindustan Unilever, I learned the principles and practise of business and management. The learning was focused on transactional leadership—getting your teeth into a problem or challenge, thinking up alternative ways to solve the problem or overcome the obstacle, rallying a group of people to execute a solution and then making a go at delivering the solution. Transactional leadership ranged from delivering sales targets for a set of company products in a national region, to increasing the company's exports to other countries. I cut my teeth as an area manager in Karnataka with a soaps and detergents portfolio, led the national business of the company's foods business before leading the audacious exports drive of the company—audacious because the company had to earn 10 per cent of its sales revenue from exports at a time when India's exports were under 2 per cent of the Gross Domestic Product (GDP).

BALCONY OF CORPORATE LEADERSHIP

In the next fifteen years of my career, mostly at Unilever, I learnt about the multidimensional tasks of running a company. At Unilever Arabia in Jeddah, it involved engagement with the many stakeholders in the firm—the principal shareholder, eleven local Arab partners, a very multinational team of managers and employees in the company, the government and society. The lessons of this phase include executing on strategy and actions for a vision that the principal shareholders had enunciated. For example, in Arabia, Unilever had a vision to challenge Procter & Gamble (P&G), its principal detergent competitor frontally. I led the crack team to lead this audacious assault—with mixed results, I should add, with the benefit of hindsight!

Arabia was a geography where, for historical reasons, Unilever had a zero share of the detergent market and the rest of the market share was with P&G. Unilever and P&G slugged it out in many parts of the world in a ding-dong battle of raids and counter-attacks—for example, in Europe and America. However, in most emerging markets, one or the other held a position of imposing dominance. In India, Indonesia, and Latin America, for example, Unilever was absolutely dominant, while in Arabia, P&G had an upper hand. It was into this field of unequal power that Unilever Arabia was sent to battle. Needless to add, Unilever had several other advantages in Arabia and an operational war chest was provided by the shareholders, so, while the task was challenging, it was not life-threatening.

R. GOPALAKRISHNAN

BALCONY OF HOLISTIC LEADERSHIP

The last fifteen years were rich with learnings and experiences in holistic leadership. Most of this period was in Tata. For the role and position that I had in Tata, the operational and transactional responsibilities rested for the most part with the CEOs of the companies. They, along with their teams, came up with detailed execution plans, held intensive review meetings and answered to the board on how well the company team had delivered on its committed targets. I had the privilege of sitting on some of the boards, observing and contributing to the process of visioning and monitoring, encouraging and supporting company leaders in their endeavours, and exploring the environment in which the company was operating. In a sense, I had a perch from where I could observe a corporation in its larger sphere of working—the deep philosophies of why the corporation exists, the industry atmospherics, the government and regulatory environment, the pulls and pressures of governance and competition, and the complex art of sharing with company leaders an exploration of higher orbits of strategy.

One of my important experiences was that I was taken quite seriously by policymakers and industry compatriots. I was hugely privileged, not because I was smart, but because I worked in Tata. It was a tradition in Tata that the group's leaders would play an important role in national economic development over several decades. I was one of the inheritors of that mantle.

My earlier books were from the first two balconies, based on my experiences and learnings at the transactional and corporate leadership levels. However, in the evening of my professional career of over half a century in management, I have now felt an urge to doodle about the view from the third balcony of holistic leadership.

The dictionary definition of the word 'doodle' suggests that it is something rough, prepared absent-mindedly. Both these adjectives could well apply to this book titled *Doodles on Leadership*. This book is about engaging with leadership moments beyond the transactional and the corporate, the 'aha' moments that are concerned with more holistic problems that occur in industry, society, nation, values and people. It has been written from the perspective of observations from a different position—the balcony of holistic leadership.

A VIEW WITH A DIFFERENCE

The view from this level is quite different to the views from the balconies of transactional and corporate leadership. But in what ways?

Firstly, it is a view through the rear view mirror. It tends to be hindsight rather than foresight or an immediate view arising from the cut and thrust of the action in the field.

Secondly, it engages the mind in larger matters than the company and its operations. Why are things around us the way that they are—in the economy, in society, and in citizenship? Based on experiences, is there an alternative view that I can express? Business people should, and do, engage with such larger issues. It is among the more satisfying of the roles that business leaders can play in the wider society.

Thirdly, it offers a chance to envision the world we think our children and grandchildren should inhabit. All views of the future will be considered naïve upon the passage of time. That has not deterred men—philosophers, scientists and artists—from imagining the future, based on trends and disruptions. Why should business people not do the same?

In addition to these three reasons, what makes the view from the balcony of holistic leadership even more interesting in this book is that it covers a wide range of subjects that have engaged me during the course of my career. My belief that all of these are of deep national interest has prompted me to present them as a book that citizens may be interested in. Some of the chapters draw on my Tata experiences, but, as the book progresses, the subjects become broader.

In the first chapter, I have reflected on the House of Tata through an imaginary conversation among the first four chairmen, from 1868 until 1991. It is based on real-life incidents and statements, all verified by the Tata Archives in Pune. The Tata group is an amazing creation for several reasons. Here is an institution that has survived and grown over 150 years. Such a venerable age is itself an accomplishment at a time when the half-life of corporations and business groups is diminishing rapidly. Further, this group has been numero uno for about eighty years, during which time several studies have been published about 'top' business groups. In 1939, the colonial government published a list of the top business houses as reported in *Indian Business and Nationalist Politics*.[1] The purpose was most likely to track the companies that might have been funding the independence movement! Tata was first, with assets worth ₹62.42 crores, according to that study. Thirty years later, in 1969, the Government of India published a ranking of business groups as part of the study on monopolies as the 'Report of the industrial licensing policy enquiry committee'. Tata was still the top business group, with assets worth ₹505.36 crores. Soon thereafter, the Monopolies and Restrictive Trade Practises Act, 1969 (MRTP) legislation was enacted and, indeed, the Tata group was classified as 'monopolistic' by aggregating the commercial achievements of its independent companies. In the years after liberalization, corporate group rankings are routine and Tata still continues to be at the top. This accomplishment is amazing—and that too, without the company ever stating an aim to be India's number one business group.

I then dwell upon experiments with changing the *culture* of innovation in the Tata group as distinct from influencing

---

[1]Markovits, Claude. *Indian Business and Nationalist Politics 1931-39: the Indigenous Capitalist Class and the Rise of the Congress Party*. Cambridge University Press, 2002.

innovation processes or outcomes. It requires applicability across a wide range of business domains, from salt to software. Innovation processes and discipline constitute the more common forms of innovation initiative in companies. Changing the *culture* of innovation, or, for that matter, changing the culture of anything, is a far more complex challenge. It involves behavioural changes and patience, both of which corporations are usually short of. The setting up of—and the lessons learnt—at the Tata Group Innovation Forum (TGIF) constitute the essence of this chapter.

Staying with the Tata group, chapter 3 explores the practise of trusteeship that I experienced within the group. It allowed me to reflect on the group's practises and the true purpose of a corporation as a member of a wide society.

While many accounts about liberalization have been written by economists and policymakers, there are very few that have been written from the perspective of the micro-firm level. For the first seven years after 1991, I served as a top executive of Unilever, and, in the period after that, I served as a top executive of Tata. I witnessed first-hand, and participated in, the firm level responses to the policy changes that had gripped the nation. How did Unilever respond and how was it different from that of the Tatas? Clearly, both have done very well, but each in its own way, as we find out in chapter four in an experimental manner rather than a historical one.

The seamless transition made by both these organizations

also provides valuable lessons for the corporate world on the smooth transition of leadership. There is considerable management writing and research on leadership succession planning, but far less about predecessor planning. They are, I think, two halves of the same fruit. It takes thought and introspection to be—and to behave like—a good predecessor.

The fifth chapter concerns succession planning and touches upon aspects related to the delicate relationship between predecessor and successor.

Whether in a company or a country, I firmly believe that enterprise and innovation are promoted by decentralizing authority and empowering people. Enterprise and decentralization must become the two sides of the same coin, particularly since the centralized form of governance adopted after independence has shackled the natural enterprise of the people in 'Little India'. If India is to experience a surge in economic growth, the entrepreneurial gene in small-town India needs to be unleashed. I highlight the many initiatives that need to be taken in this direction in chapter 6.

But India's national economic growth will be significantly impacted only if it has its roots in agricultural productivity. During my long career, I had, all along, been associated with rural markets through sales of consumer products, rural development, and selling dairy and poultry feeds, as well as through marketing of seeds, agricultural chemicals and fertilizers. Listening to the budget speeches of India's Finance Ministers (FM) over many decades, I was struck by the fact that every FM, without exception, paid tribute to India's farmers and proposed economic solutions to spur farmer income. Doubtless, there was progress through, for example, the green revolution for food grains and the white revolution in dairying. Yet, agricultural productivity in India has, for a long time, been stuck at half of China's productivity. I feel that India needs to do something differently. We need a framework to transform the entire agricultural value chain, as I argue in my next chapter.

Chapter 8 concerns yet another problem that everybody is aware of, but nobody is able to change—the availability of justice for the common citizen. India ranks as belonging among the more litigious societies in the world. In the traditional manner, disputes were settled by village elders because India was, in reality, a 'government-less civilization'—a term coined by C. Rajagopalachari. Now with more modern forms of judicial processes, and a fine one at that, the citizen faces the spectre of long waits for justice.

I believe that as we promote enterprise and social justice and the world globalizes, more and more businessmen will represent India's progress and problems to outside nations and investors. If our business people feel positive despite the warts and moles that they are inevitably familiar with, an honest energy is generated in the image of India among overseas managers and investors. I call this transformation that India is attempting 'Insaniyat' (a Hindi word that means fairness or equitability, in English) and explore this in detail in chapter 9. I stick my neck out and make a prediction that the next fifteen years will be the best economic period that India has experienced in its long history of three millenniums.

In the tenth and final chapter, I reflect upon a corporate career and how it contributes to the nation and society. I explore the adage that you can earn well by doing good. I assert, based on my experiences, that good corporate management is essential to national economic growth and that business management and enterprise is a potentially satisfying career for young people in the period ahead.

1

Candid Conversations of Torchbearers and Trailblazers

Frank Harris, historian and biographer of Jamsetji Tata, recorded that a partnership firm called Tata & Sons was established in 1868. While the precise date is unclear, a good conjecture is that it was sometime between July and September 1868. With Tata Sons completing 150 years in 2018, it is only befitting that a former Director of Tata Sons Limited pays a tribute to the institution. Based on historical facts, I imagine a conversation among four former chairmen, who together led Tata from 1868 till 1991—Founder Jamsetji; his son, Dorabji; Dorabji's successor, Nowroji Saklatwala; and his successor, J.R.D. Tata.

Jamsetji: *Aao dikra.* It has been a long time since we chatted together. What we are doing today is an unusual opportunity, is it not? The company we had served has renewed itself constantly, to survive and grow. The culture and values of Tata, which have persisted for over a century, are very precious. Future leaders must know what aspects of this culture must not change and what aspects must adapt to change. However, I suggest a word of caution for our discussion: that we reminisce about our times, but we do not make judgements about our modern-day successors. They are managing a vastly different business in a vastly different world. Like you, I will always wish and pray that they are holding on to the purpose that we had set for the business, and some core values. I think Tata companies have done so for all of these years.

J.R.D.: Yes, of course, dear Kakaji. As you know, as one of your original partners in the business, my father (R.D.) would harangue me periodically about your vision and how you had ever so endearingly articulated the purpose of the firm. You had said that the firm is an integral part of the community, and it exists to serve the community. Eighty years later, during the 1960s, when I was the chairman, I said pretty much the same thing in the business language of my times: what the firm earns from the people must go back to the people, many times over. It is good that this strong foundation and our business purpose have both remained intact, although the profile and appurtenances of the business have changed. There will always be challenging times and apparent aberrations, but I am sure that the true purpose of the firm continues to be what we had intended, articulated and practised.

Dorabji: It is wonderful to know that our current generation is able to maintain our corporate purpose—that too, consistently for over a century. Among the four of us, we have experienced 150 years of the firm: colonial India, the 1930s depression, two World Wars, partition, the independence of our beloved nation, global economic cycles, and an explosion in the population of India.

Jamsetji: Yes, that is true, but the intrinsic challenges of running a business surely have remained broadly similar. I remember what a tough time I had when I bought Dharamsi Mills in Kurla, later renamed as Svadeshi Mills, because the idea of making things in India appealed to me. I was convinced that such acquisitions at a low price must be seriously considered; if I could buy an asset for cheap, I felt I had a decent chance to turn it around by making finer products than it did before. Really, it was nerve racking because the Tata name was at stake. I staked my own wealth and even broke the Trusts to raise the funds required.

Dorabji: Papa, you are so right about what happens when the name Tata is at stake. You may recall that you were so indisposed at Bad Nauheim, cousin R.D. and I came to meet you. You said to us about your wealth, 'If you cannot make it greater, at least preserve it. Do not let things slide. Go on doing my work and increasing it, but if you cannot, do not lose what we have already done.' We could not raise capital from the London market, but Indian financiers surprised us by subscribing to the capital of our steel company. After initial troubles, the company made its first ingot of steel in 1912. Within four years, I told shareholders of my plan to expand the steel production because in 1916, I told the shareholders about the bumper earnings due to production of 30 per cent above designed capacity, breaking order books and ready markets! However, World War I began, transport and labour costs spiralled out of control, and an earthquake struck Japan, the biggest pig iron market. Our steel company was suddenly staring down an abyss.

J.R.D.: Oh yes Dorabji, my father had told me this story. Was this not the occasion when one of the directors suggested that the government take over the steel mill? My father said he was livid and that he thumped the table, swearing that this would not happen so long as he was alive!

Dorabji: Yes indeed, Jeh, your father did. After that episode of thumping the table, we received a telegram from Jamshedpur stating that there was inadequate money to pay the wages of employees. I went to the Imperial Bank of India and pledged my wife's jewellery to secure a loan. After that,

Papa's adopted motto for the firm, *Humata, Hukta, Huvarsta* (Good thoughts, words and deeds) worked well because Ahura Mazda (The Lord) smiled, and our fortunes turned.

J.R.D.: Yes Dorabji. Even the Taj Mahal hotel, which was one of kaka's dream projects, took ever so long to make a profit. They used to call it the 'Tata White Elephant'. I found a talented hotelier in Ajit Kerkar, who turned the Taj around brilliantly. During my chairmanship, we acquired a soda ash business at Mithapur. People even told me that we had bought the wrong business in the wrong place. Thanks to the imaginative leadership of another professional, Darbari Seth, the business turned round. I understand that Tata is now the world's second largest soda ash player.

Saklatwala: Yeah, what you folks say is true; yet, there can be exceptions to the situation. You must try very hard to turn around acquisitions or new ventures. But if, after trying hard and sincerely, you fail—maybe for market-driven reasons—then you also need to stop the haemorrhage. How long can you persist with operations that you are simply unable to turn around? How do you judge when to call it quits? After our time, Tata Textiles and Tata Oil Mills were divested because Tata could not see a way to make a sustainable success of it.

Dorabji: Indeed, you raise a valid issue. I think you have to do everything you possibly can with a great degree of sincerity—and then the time comes to take a call. After 1917, I launched eleven new ventures; in each of them, investors fought to get shares—such was the faith in the Tata name. Apart from Tata Oil Mills, I set up Tata Industrial Bank, New India Assurance Company, Tata Construction, Tata Electro-Chemicals, Tata Sugar Corporation—just to name a few. Market conditions were tough, and some of the ventures ran into problems.

Saklatwala: Indeed, and when I succeeded you, Dorabji, I had to get a grip on the situation I faced. The firm was over-leveraged and the global recession did not help. Your decisions may have been right when you took them, but later developments had their own impact. I expressed my thoughts in a speech, 'Those were truly mad days, and perhaps the maddest feature was the supreme confidence of the public in Tata, and, incidentally, the overconfidence of Tata themselves.' I really felt that these ventures suffered from insufficient preparation before their inception; some of them were over-capitalized in anticipation of rapid expansion, and some from a rapid collapse of market values and prices.

Dorabji: Yes, my dear Nowroji; I did hear the stories about those property disposals, but luckily for you, I was not around to express any views! Times have changed, and nowadays businesses are sold and bought, hopefully with grace and fairness. I heard that after the times when we headed the group, the Tata Sons board has periodically debated which businesses should be divested and how. But, to be fair, I did support new businesses as well. Jeh—as I recall, I supported you entering the airline business around 1929.

J.R.D.: Dorabji, in the late 1920s, you were totally against my idea of entering the airline business. You felt that we were too stretched at that time, both financially and managerially. The Tata Sons board minutes clearly carried the message of the board rejecting the firm's entry into airlines. So I went to my mentor—John Peterson, you remember him? I cried out my emotions to him.

Dorabji: You did put Peterson on to me. How he pleaded for you. He said something like, 'Let the young man fly with his dreams.' Finally I relented, and you did a great job of developing Tata Airlines. It was one business which you developed personally and could take full credit for. But Jeh, you were ever so keen about the airline, it must have broken your heart to let it go when the government nationalized it.

J.R.D.: In fact, more than nationalization, it was the way I was removed from chairmanship that hurt me. In business, one must take the decision that is felt to be right, but one must also attempt to implement it gracefully. However, once the government decided to remove me from Air India, I swallowed my pride and accepted it.

Jamsetji: Changing the track slightly to development of business leaders, Jeh, you referred to Ajit Kerkar and Darbari Seth as great leaders. I learnt early on that the key to my enterprise would be to find the right people to run the businesses. I recruited an extraordinary man called Bezonji Mehta, a self-made man who had worked in the railways. I trained him and he responded very well. Later, when I went into steel, I walked the streets of London and New York to find technocrats. It was not that I always sought foreign technicians. For the Taj architecture, I consulted Sitaram Khanderao Vaidya. Only after he died, did I bring in W.A. Chambers.

J.R.D.: Kakaji, I think you make an exceptional point about developing technocrats and managers. India had no business managers in those days, so Tata had to develop them internally through mentoring, as well as through real-life and hands-on experience. Many Tata leaders went on to public positions. When India was partitioned, Prime Minister Liaquat Ali Khan of Pakistan appointed Sir Malik Ghulam Muhammad, who was a Tata director, as the new nation's first Finance Minister. Jawaharlal Nehru, Prime Minister of the new Indian government, asked that Tata director Sir John Mathai join the Interim Cabinet—first, to be the Railway Minister, and later to be the second Finance Minister in the Union Cabinet. A.D. Shroff and Nani Palkhivala were two doyens on the Tata Sons board who were as influential as

Finance Ministers without ever becoming Finance Ministers. When young Sumant Moolgaokar joined the Tata board, he remarked, 'At the lunch table, you felt that Tata belonged to the nation.'

Dorabji: This is an important part of Tata history. Jeh, you have rattled off many names of exceptional business leaders, and perhaps you, more than any of us, needed all of them in free, independent India. Sumant Moolgaokar in engineering, Faqir Chand Kohli in power and computers—how on earth did you attract them, and lead them?

J.R.D.: You know, early on, I realized that I could not possibly manage all these businesses by myself. I realized that I was no genius. Further, my technical education was nipped in the bud because dad asked me to join the business as early as 1924. So I went right out, looking for people who would be better than I was. I consciously gave them the space and visibility to stretch and deliver to their full potential. We had differences, but after some discussion and arguments, I let them do things their way. In this regard, I particularly recall A.D. Shroff, a hugely talented economist, but also given to strong opinions. I managed to get the best out of him for the nation and for Tata. What would be the use of recruiting them and then subjugating them to my view, which had its own limitations?

Jamsetji: Well, well, I must say that it is a great credit to you that you could do this. A true leader, I reckon, is one who is not so insecure that he needs to impose his views on others arising out of his status or position. True power must emanate from listening to others and from a display of warmth. Authoritativeness and leadership emanate, not necessarily from status, but from these qualities. It sure is tough to do that.

Saklatwala: Well, this has been a great conversation. All of us can feel happy that the institution which we all served and built continues to prosper. I pray that it continues into the future.

Jamsetji: I join you in your prayer. Like human beings, organizations too need renewal. Just one individual could have the power to renew an institution and elevate it to the expectations of the founding fathers if he has two qualities: first, he should have no past to hide, and second, he should have no personal expectation for the future.

The firm created by Jamsetji Tata has completed 150 years of business in India and overseas, and is one of India's most prominent long-lasting business institutions.

2

Innovation in its DNA

It was a surprisingly pleasant June morning in 2015, but something seemed amiss to Ravi Arora, Vice President Innovation at Tata Sons as he sat across the table from me. I had chaired the Tata Group Innovation Forum (TGIF) for a little under a decade by then, and I knew that with my impending retirement, I was about to move on from that position. Ravi Arora had been my closest co-worker in TGIF during that period. After offering Arora a cup of the freshly brewed coffee that rested on the antique cedar wood table in the office on the top floor of Bombay House (in Mumbai), I said:

> TGIF is a decade old this month. While we must commemorate its tenth anniversary, I often wonder if it has met the board's objective of creating organizational cultures in the group companies that would encourage

the emergence of disruptive technologies. Have we truly been able to catalyze innovations that group companies may want to adopt? Should we leave innovation to the individual companies or should we continue to have a centralized innovation function in the form of TGIF? How effective has TGIF been in the group and what is its future?

While formulating a response in his head, Arora was reminded of the various points of view that people had shared with him about TGIF. Putting down his coffee, he drew my attention to the focal question on which the future of a set-up like TGIF pivoted—for a conglomerate, how much should the holding company do to advance innovation in the group without interfering in operating companies? He said:

> Many group companies do not focus on innovation, as they are busy achieving targets. This short term view clashes with Tata Sons' (the holding company) long term view. But how much should Tata Sons do? What's the balance? Till 2005, we focused on only encouraging the operating companies. After 2006, we have been running programs where we expect these companies to participate. Some people are of the view that we are just singing and dancing and not having a very serious impact, since TGIF does not have a clear measure or indicator of results. Another school of thought believes that Tata Sons should not interfere

in operating companies and should do things slow and steady so that they are sustainable.

Adding another layer to my initial question about TGIF's future, Arora reminded me of the constant dilemma that TGIF faced while supporting innovations—should culture (making the ground fertile) be given more focus over process or should it be vice-versa? These were two absolutely opposite views.

A GLOBAL ICON RISES

The Tata group, which came to be called Tata Sons, was founded by a young 29-year-old Jamsetji Nusserwanji Tata in 1868. Though young in age, he had sharp business acumen, the credit for which belonged to the hands-on experience in business that his father gave him while Jamsetji assisted him at a trading company in Bombay (now Mumbai). Jamsetji's indelible contribution to industrialization in India was apparent in the number of businesses that the Tata group pioneered across varied sectors. After Jamsetji died in 1904, the mantle of Tata Sons was taken over by his son Dorabji Tata who worked towards fulfilling his father's dream of making India a developed country. The group, with its far sighted leaders, had many firsts to its credit.

In 1938, Tata Sons got its longest serving chairman in the form of J.R.D. Tata, who steered the group through the difficult times that fell upon industry in independent India.

After India's independence in 1947, the Indian government strictly controlled businesses. Despite the deceleration in innovations due to tight government control, the Tata group, under JRD's leadership, grew rapidly.

The early 1990s brought in several changes in Indian business. The economic reforms of 1991 opened up many sectors, signalling increased competition and the arrival of foreign companies. Owing to J.R.D's illness (he died in 1993), the mantle of leading the Tata group through the fast-changing business environment, where new realities were taking shape, was given to Ratan Tata. He took over as group chairman in 1991 and brought about big changes by rejuvenating existing businesses and entering new ones, making acquisitions, engineering breakthrough products, and expanding into foreign markets during his tenure.

By the early 2000s, some of the group companies had established their position in the Indian market, and others were on their way to becoming global. It was at this time that the Tata group identified that 'innovation' should be the key focus area and made a serious effort to approach it more systematically.

The future promised plenty for the Tata group as it set the agenda for the next phase of its evolution. Ratan Tata had remarked:

> One hundred years from now, I expect the Tatas to be much bigger, of course, than it is now. More importantly, I hope the group comes to be regarded as

being the best in India—best in the manner in which we operate, best in the products we deliver and best in our value system and ethics. Having said that, I hope that a hundred years from now we will spread our wings far beyond India, that we become a global group, operating in many countries, an Indian business conglomerate that is at home in the world, carrying the same sense of trust that we do today.

CREATING AN INNOVATION ECOSYSTEM

Although the group had showcased so many examples of innovations over the last century, the prevailing perception internally and externally in 2005, was that the group was not innovative and had not done enough work towards innovation. At that time, I was entrusted with the responsibility of exploring how the organizational culture of innovation could be improved. Whether the Tata group's lack of innovativeness was just a perception or had some objective basis was a moot point.

To support the Tata companies in their respective journeys of innovation, the Tata Group Innovation Forum (TGIF) was set up in 2007 under my leadership. TGIF comprised of CEOs/CXOs and Innovation Champions from different Tata companies. TGIF met every quarter to review and intensify its efforts towards creating an innovation ecosystem.

The Forum's objective was set as: 'To encourage, inspire

and help create a culture, which would foster innovation in the companies.' To achieve this goal, the forum devised a three-pronged charter—encourage Tata companies to create an environment that supported innovation, advise Tata companies on improving innovation capability, and create a group-wide community of innovation evangelists.

TGIF focused on developing new concepts and tools that would help companies measure their innovativeness as well as handle related culture and leadership matters. It focused on establishing processes to generate and execute innovative ideas and created a Rewards and Recognition system for innovation.

Tata Quality Management Services (TQMS, later renamed as Tata Business Excellence Group) was chosen as the implementation arm of TGIF. A five member team, led by Arora, was appointed to facilitate the TGIF discussions and implement the action items identified during these discussions. The innovation team was absolved of all other activities of TQMS. (The main role of TQMS was to drive the Tata Business Excellence program in Tata companies.)

TGIF encouraged, nurtured and executed ideas centrally and in Tata companies. The Forum introduced a number of initiatives that would build capabilities, enhance the culture of innovation and inspire managers, for example:

Demystifying innovation

TGIF regularly invited academicians like Prof. Clayton Christensen from Harvard Business School, Prof. Henry

Chesbrough from University of California at Berkeley, Prof. Julian Birkinshaw from London Business School, Prof. William Ouchi, University of California at Los Angeles and innovation experts like Dr James Canton, CEO and Chairman, Institute for Global Futures, San Francisco and Langdon Morris, Partner at Innovation Labs, Systematic Inventive Thinking (SIT—Israel), IDEO, Mckinsey to conduct workshops that would help Tata companies understand the concept of innovation, to introduce new concepts and tools, and to stimulate innovative thinking among managers. These programmes significantly enhanced the knowledge base on innovation within the group. In addition, the Tata Management Training Centre (TMTC), with the help of internationally renowned experts, continuously built capability in group companies.

The Forum organized several innovation learning missions in some of the most innovative companies in the world for managers. These missions were introduced to help group companies understand the practises followed by innovative companies in countries like the US, Japan and Israel.

To ensure a positive and major change within the group, knowledge gained through these visits was shared in detail within the group. TMTC regularly organized programmes to disseminate information and knowledge meant to institutionalize a culture of innovation within the Tata companies. Some of the executive leadership programmes organized by TMTC, with the help of Harvard and Michigan universities, had a special focus on innovation. In addition, TMTC regularly published and circulated research outcomes on innovation.

Encouraging innovation

Early on, TGIF realized that the best way to encourage innovation was to create stories and recognize people who were responsible behind the scenes. This led to the institutionalization of innovation awards called Tata InnoVista, which was rebranded in 2007 after the initial launch of Tata Innovation Day the previous year.

This programme had multiple objectives: to recount all the previous innovations of Tata companies and use the stories to instill self-confidence among Tata managers, in order to trigger new ideas in different situations; to recognize innovators and encourage innovations in companies; to build a culture of appropriate risk taking; and to share and learn the levers used by companies to identify and execute innovation projects.

Teams from all the Tata companies could participate in the regional rounds of InnoVista, held in seven regions—New Delhi, Mumbai, Bengaluru, Kolkata, London, New Jersey and Singapore. The projects at these centres were reviewed by both Tata and non-Tata jurors. The winners were invited to participate in the finals in Mumbai. The finalists were judged by a panel of non-Tata jurors, including accomplished personalities like Dr R.A. Mashelkar, former Director General of the Council of Scientific and Industrial Research; (CSIR) Dr K Kasturirangan, former Chairman of the Indian Space Research Organisation (ISRO); Arun Maira, Member of the Planning Commission, and Kiran Karnik, former Chief, Nasscom. The winners received awards from the Tata Sons Group Chairman. Participation in Tata InnoVista grew rapidly over the years—the 101 entries in 2006 had shot up to 2800 in 2015.

In 2010, TGIF launched Tata Ideas, a crowd-sourcing platform that could be the ideation hub for all Tata companies. Through this platform, Tata employees could share, collaborate, predict and implement innovative ideas. People could then share, vote, like, bet and comment on ideas before the decision to select or reject them was taken. The platform allowed Tata leaders to list out their challenges. This was perhaps one of the first IT applications that cut across many Tata companies in which transactions (around ideas) were done. By 2017, this system was being used by twelve Tata companies for creative problem solving. The success of Tata Ideas led to the beginning of a new experiment, 'Challenges worth Solving (CWS)', in which a few Tata companies listed out difficult challenges twice a year to seek creative solutions.

It was observed that 58 per cent of the ideas received to solve a challenge were from the company that listed the challenge. This number was reduced to 30 per cent for CWS.

For CWS, the best ideas received a special award during the Tata InnoVista awards ceremony.

Another platform, Implement Ideas (earlier known as InnoCompass), was created to ensure that the winning ideas were implemented and their status was visible to relevant people. This was a lean stage-gate process which allowed every idea to define its stage and gate, and allowed the leader of the team to define separate teams for every stage. Additionally, it enabled the company to capture the rich knowledge that was generated during project implementation. This tool also presented the innovation portfolio or the innovation dashboard to the company or the business unit in question, which could be used to take proactive steps to strengthen it.

Workshops, based on the concepts of Prof. Clayton Christensen, were conducted under the title of 'InnoMultiplier'. These workshops helped the company identify innovation opportunities and challenges. The well-known concept of 'jobs to be done' was extensively used in this workshop to identify opportunities. The participants were exposed to several other tools and were taken through ethnographic immersive exercises to observe and listen to customers. The opportunities identified through the InnoMultiplier exercise were added to the Innovation portfolio. Those identified through the workshops were broken down into smaller challenges. Some of these challenges were thrown open on the Tata Ideas platform for others to solve.

Measuring innovation

TGIF used a simple and easy-to-use tool, InnoMeter, to measure the innovativeness of a team, a business unit, a department or a company. This unique tool was developed after consideration of the extensive research on the various methods available to measure innovation. Prof Julian Birkinshaw of the London Business School had the most inputs on the final design. InnoMeter showed the health of the innovation ecosystem of an organization and helped determine its state under three dimensions—innovation process, innovation culture, and strategic focus for innovation.

I consider Innometer to be a comprehensive innovation health check which is as reflective as a mirror and stimulates companies to work on improving their innovativeness. It also showcases how innovative they are when compared to a set of benchmark companies and informs the company whether it is outside the band on any of the attributes under the three dimensions.

The Innometer study was conducted in around twenty-five Tata companies from the metals, chemicals, service, engineering, consumer goods and telecom sectors. The study collated qualitative and quantitative feedback using surveys and discussions.

In 2009, a study was conducted on the 'State of Innovation' in thirteen Tata companies. Around 2000 managers were covered. In 2010, a similar study was conducted for Tata companies in Europe. One of the major findings of both these studies was that most managers, of almost every company, lacked full awareness of the innovative work within their company. This indicated the need for more programmes that recognized and celebrated the organization's innovation efforts.

EXPLORING NEW AVENUES

Collaborative innovation

The diversified Tata group used to have only a few companies that invested in Research & Technology (R&T). There was no mechanism or structure to bring companies together to explore new avenues of innovation using R&T inputs. Further, the learning missions to the US and Japan proved that innovative ideas were more likely to get triggered when people from different industries and backgrounds came together.

As a preparatory measure towards establishing the need for bringing R&T professionals together, an exercise was undertaken in 2007 to seek the opinions of personnel across the group on key issues that hindered such synergistic efforts. Another aim of the exercise was to get possible remedies to the issues identified by them. Based on the conversations with the concerned personnel, including the MDs, CEOs, R&D/Technology heads, junior researchers and technologists, it was found that professionals working in R&D were ignorant about the capabilities and potentials of other group companies. Several companies adopted technology (bought or acquired through joint ventures), as development of new technology was not one of their priorities. Moreover, most companies focused on achieving marginally higher productivity, which required only minor improvements in technology. These companies hardly paid any attention to generating Intellectual Property Rights (IPR). As a result of the lack of challenging projects, several talented engineers and scientists left the R&D departments of the operating companies. Many stated that they would be interested in cross-functional and cross-technology projects, as those would provide them an opportunity to work in newer areas.

Another finding from the discussions with people from different companies was that the smaller companies within a business sector (there were seven business sectors in the Tata group) that depended on bigger companies in the same business sector for R&T often did not get priority.

In a meeting in 2008, attended by the chief technology/research officers of thirteen Tata companies, it was decided that opportunities for technological innovations should be explored through the formation of clusters of Tata companies in related businesses. This created the concept of InnoClusters, which was regarded as amongst the most promising, enticing and challenging initiatives of TGIF.

InnoClusters were conceptualized to leverage existing capabilities and technologies in order to enhance and innovate through the group's products and services, and also solve current technical problems, brainstorm to conceive a few larger innovation projects that could be possible only by collaboration among companies (and maybe alongside institutes), and bring more focus on R&T within companies.

The idea of an InnoCluster was to leverage the infrastructural and intellectual strengths of technical experts in various Tata companies for innovative projects in select areas. The three types of clusters included thematic clusters with only Tata companies as participants (for example, nanotechnology, water, information and communication technology), those between Tata companies and external enterprises (for example, Dupont, Corning, 3M, P&G), and those between Tata companies and a technical institute (for example Fraunhofer).

This programmed method to strike and nurture collaborations was dropped from the agenda of TGIF after the Tata group created the CTO forum, which met twice a year with a similar purpose.

Open innovation

In 2009, Prof. Henry Chesbrough advised TGIF to start practicing Open Innovation, i.e., breaching group boundaries to find the best solutions. TGIF tried hard to devise a few challenges that could be given to Open Innovation intermediaries like Innocentive and NineSigma. However, no company was ready to share a challenge. They were either concerned about sharing confidential information with the external world, or were not ready to accept that they could not solve their own problems.

Five years later, the innovation team carried out an experiment by taking three challenges from Tata companies and assigning them to an intermediary. The results exceeded our internal expectations and, as a result, the TGIF decided to expand this practise as some TGIF members, including myself, wanted it to expand.

Redesigning what it means to be innovative

Just before coming to my office, Arora had picked up a copy of the detailed assessment report on TGIF that was submitted in early 2015 by Dr Phanish Puranam, the Roland Berger Chair Professor of Strategy & Organization Design at INSEAD Business School. Since Arora had gone through the report in detail, he referred to it to answer my initial question regarding TGIF's future. He first discussed the positives about TGIF, as indicated in the report, and said:

> According to Dr Puranam, TGIF was successful in inculcating two key ideas relating to the democratization of innovation: that innovation was not restricted to R&D departments and that it could come from anywhere in the hierarchy as well as from outside the company's boundaries. The scope of TGIF's initiatives mapped well onto the basic types of democratized (i.e. non-R&D) innovation programmes seen in global

corporations: reward and recognition (InnoVista), contests (Challenges worth Solving) and online collaboration programmes (Innoverse).

Though I was happy, I was concerned about some of the observations and action points mentioned in the report. I asked Arora to focus on the following select points that, according to me, required immediate attention:

- The potential for 'open innovation' that involved breaching the boundaries of the group was largely unrealized. It appeared that there was no initiative designed to tap 'lead users' as a source of innovation.
- Of the three main active initiatives of TGIF, InnoVista had achieved a high and stable level of penetration with 50-60 per cent of the group companies participating every year. InnoMeter and Innoverse had far lower adoption rates of 15-20 per cent. These could be improved through a data-backed elucidation of benefits, but it might be unrealistic to expect adoption rates in the operating model to approach those of InnoVista, for certain structural reasons.
- It was difficult to point to a disruptive innovation or technology that could be attributed directly to the TGIF initiatives. In fact, it was unrealistic that disruptive innovations be expected from TGIF initiatives.

- Data collection on the consequences of TGIF initiatives could be improved. In particular, process related metrics on Innoverse, and before-after measures of innovation outcomes for companies that go through the InnoMeter exercise, should be collected.
- We could consider certain fundamental changes in the operating model—to decentralize and customize, depending on the company—some of the activities being conducted as TGIF initiatives, get each company to define its own sector-relevant metrics of innovation and finally integrate the first two within an appropriate reporting framework.

I was keen that TGIF should focus on these health indicators from the report and evaluate options to resolve them. At the end of the hour long meeting with me, Arora picked up his copy of Dr Puranam's report, on which he had scribbled some notes while highlighting the following points:

- Change TGIF's mandate to include program management of projects to ensure that ideas selected are implemented.
- Increase the implementation team to work closer and be engaged with Tata companies for a longer period.
- Delve deeper into figuring how to start open innovation.

As Arora walked out of my office, he knew that a revamp

of TGIF was on the cards, and he had to figure out two things—the aspects of Dr Puranam's observations that could be implemented and the manner in which to do that.

Thus, while there was an air of celebration within the TGIF team (given the tenth anniversary), Arora could sense that if it had to continue to exist, TGIF had to think of some serious innovation. Welcome to the future.

3

Tradition of Trusteeship

The business world today is at an inflection point. At the time of the industrial revolution, the basis of competitive advantage for the business world was industrial assets or physical assets. In the last thirty years, we have heard a lot about competitiveness being based on information assets or knowledge assets. As we go forward into whatever the next age will be called, I wonder whether the basis will be ethical assets.

I realize that this sounds rather pompous, but I can't help feeling that there is enough evidence around us in society today to justify exploring such an idea. After all, commerce and business are predicated on the principles of capitalism, and it doesn't matter where in the world you go—capitalism is associated with greed, avarice, ego and all sorts of negative qualities.

Excesses have happened periodically throughout the history of commerce. Ever since the Joint Stock Company was invented in 1856, the facts of such excesses have been recorded. Considering that excesses seem to be rampant today, it may be prudent to reflect on what the future might be.

There are two factors that we need to consider. First, that the Joint Stock Company is here to stay as a major agent of change in social and economic development in all sorts of societies and countries around the world. Second, that there are more and more individuals in society who are driven by a set of personal values, which represent what they stand for and how they would work. They may work in a company which creates its own corporate environment and culture; that culture may be at variance with their personal values. They struggle to reconcile these two. In other words, there is mutuality—an increasing nexus between the personal values of an individual and the corporate values of the entity through which he or she earns his or her living.

These are two factors we cannot run away from, and both are important for the future. This aspect can be better understood with two episodes from a completely different arena, far away from business—mountaineering.

THE MOUNTAINEER'S DILEMMA

In 1982, a senior executive in Morgan Stanley, New York, Bowen McCoy, undertook a six-month sabbatical which was sponsored by his company. A mountaineering expedition in the Himalayas was part of that sabbatical, in order to achieve greater self-awareness and knowledge about himself. McCoy and another colleague of his almost reached the end and were just a little short of the last assault on the target peak that they had set out to conquer. Following behind them was a New Zealand team of mountaineers, and behind them, a Japanese group. They had reached a very important point, from where the final assault would begin.

As McCoy, his colleague and the porters set out on this last assault, they heard a groan from the ice around them. They found the body of a sadhu, who was naked, ill-equipped for the minus 38 degrees temperature, at an altitude of 18,000 feet. The sadhu seemed to be dying. This gave rise to a dilemma. Should all of them abandon the expedition and go back with the sadhu to save his life? Should they carry the sadhu with them to the peak? Should some of them take the sadhu back and some go ahead with the expedition?

McCoy's individual values, which must have undoubtedly been benign, religious, and fraternal, required him to save a fellow being. That task should have been put on highest priority. But the group's mountaineering attitude, laced with the competitive desire to reach the mountain peak, argued that the sadhu may live or die, but they must definitely achieve their goal.

Finally, they left the sadhu and went on to conquer the peak. It is not clear whether the sadhu lived or died.

McCoy wrote it up as a case, which the Harvard Business School has published. It is about the ethical dilemma that this posed to him and to his colleague. McCoy revealed that until his dying day, the issue of his own role in determining whether the sadhu would survive or die would continue to haunt him. He was not able to reconcile his individual value system with the ambitions of the mountaineer's value system into which he found himself incorporated.

Had the mountaineers reached a consensus through discussions on what had to be done, his conscience might have rested easier. As it happened, they did not work out a consensus.

In 2007, there was another mountaineering episode. This one involved a mountain climbing event for disabled people. Mark Inglis, a double amputee from New Zealand, achieved a remarkable feat by climbing Mount Everest. However, as it so happened, on his way up Inglis found one man of his forty member team, David Sharp, dying. Inglis had to choose between helping Sharp and going ahead with climbing the mountain. He chose to climb the mountain. It became a subject of great controversy on the subject of ethics and human values. So, despite the great achievement of climbing Everest as a double amputee, his feat became controversial on the grounds of ethics.

I mention these two stories because they bring out, in a non-corporate context, the kind of conflicts we face every day in reconciling our individual value system and the organizational value system, in negotiating our values within the value system into which we are placed. This happens all the time when we operate in business. My instinct tells me one thing, but my company environment suggests another. Finding harmony between the corporate value system, which I influence through my behaviour, and my personal value system, which the corporation influences through its behaviour, is an essential part of understanding the true nature of business.

Business is not merely commerce; it has a humane aspect to it. The events around the world today suggest that we tend to forget this. In the Tatas, we have had several such experiences within the realm of corporate trusteeship and the group's tradition of trust.

'SERVANT LEADERSHIP' REDEFINED

The first lesson that I learnt is that business is a servant to society and not the other way around. If you observe how business leaders behave, you might get the feeling that business controls society.

In the late 1800s, Swami Vivekananda went to Chicago to attend the Parliament of Religions. He became a very ardent and outspoken advocate of human values. One of the people he met in Chicago was John D. Rockefeller, who had made a great fortune in the booming oil business at that time. Rockefeller was introduced to Swami Vivekananda by a French woman disciple. She wrote about their meeting in her diary.

Rockefeller probably came for a lark; he had been told that a saffron-clad monk was electrifying the people of Chicago, and it is possible that he went out of curiosity and wasn't really interested in meeting Swami Vivekananda. Swamiji didn't even look up from his desk when Rockefeller entered. He continued to do his work. After a while, he looked up at his visitor, who was not really used to being treated like a commoner. He took his seat and a conversation ensued. It became apparent to Swamiji that Rockefeller was very wealthy. Swamiji posed him a question, 'If you have that much more money than other people, do you think you are that much smarter than the others too?' Rockefeller replied in the affirmative. After all, if he wasn't a hundred times smarter, he wouldn't have a hundred times more money, would he? Swamiji impressed on him that perhaps he was not one hundred times smarter, but merely three times smarter. If he had made a hundred times more money by being just three times smarter than others, then perhaps he was merely an instrument through which this money had to go back to somebody else? Swamiji urged Rockefeller to consider leaving some of his money for other people.

This sounded absolutely ridiculous to Rockefeller, and he departed with the polite statement that he had worked really hard to make his money. He had absolutely no intention of leaving it to other people. But curiously, three weeks later, he came back to see Swami Vivekananda, this time of his own accord. He threw on his table a piece of paper, through which he had endowed a certain sum of money (it was small by Rockefeller's standards) for some noble purpose. He asked Swamiji, 'Are you happy now that I have done this?' Swamiji responded, 'Why should I be happy? You have to ask yourself the question—have you given enough out of the total wealth that you have?'

It took another fifteen years—until 1913—for John D. Rockefeller to set up the Rockefeller Foundation, which has done an enormous amount of good work in society for the last several decades. The element of trusteeship comes out so clearly in this conversation between Swamiji and Rockefeller. When you have earned a lot of money, whose money is it? Did that money come to you entirely because of yourself, or is it possible that you are merely an instrument through which you should channelize it back to society? These are very interesting questions to ponder.

TATA'S COMMITMENT TOWARDS TRUSTEESHIP

When I joined Tata in 1998, I learned the fact that probably the world's first charitable trust was set up by Jamsetji Tata in 1892, a long time before the Rockefeller Trust, the Andrew Carnegie Trust, the Ford Foundation, and the Leverhulme Trust, all of which came in the 1900s. So what made Jamsetji, who was wealthy by Indian standards of the

1880s, but probably not so by international standards, set up an instrument—the J.N. Tata Endowment Trust—that was not well known or widely practised by companies at that time? As he articulated its purpose, it would enable talented Indians to go abroad to get advanced training so that they could return to India to work for the betterment of their country.

He was firmly of the belief that if you want to advance a society, you need good people to become better people, and finally become the best. As it so happens that between 1892 and today, the J.N. Tata Trust has sent over 3,000 Indians abroad. Of the many illustrious alumni, one of them became a Chairman of the Atomic Energy Commission, another, a Director General of the Council of Scientific and Industrial Research, and a third, the President of India.

If you nurture good people and allow them to become better—or the best—they can play very significant roles in the nation's economic development. Pakistan got its first Finance Minister, Ghulam Muhammad, from the Tata boardroom after Prime Minister Liaquat Ali Khan called J.R.D. Tata to seek his agreement in offering the job to J.R.D's colleague. India got a Railway Minister—who later became the Finance Minister—from the Tata boardroom in the form of John Mathai. India found an Ambassador to the USA in the Tata boardroom when Nani Palkhivala went on to perform that role. All of these are examples to illustrate how business can be the servant of society.

The ulterior motive behind making profits is not merely to declare a dividend or bonus shares. As J.R.D. said, what came from the people must go back to the people. Who does the company earn its profits from? From the capital given by shareholders, and consumers, and accrued from trade with vendors, using transport contractors and so on. If there is some surplus, who does that surplus belong to? Not just to the shareholders—it belongs to whole community, the whole society. In this global world, this means that what comes from the six and a half billion consumers of the world must, in some way, go back to the six and a half billion consumers of the world. Thus, the fundamental characteristic of working with the trusteeship concept concerns the real purpose of business—to return to society what you earn from it.

A LEADER'S PRIVILEGE, NOT HIS PLIGHT

If you are going it to return it to society, you must work with a certain attitude that was described by Lord Leverhulme. Lord Leverhulme founded Unilever, Britain's largest company, and in so doing, made the first modern multinational. He believed that the task of a leader is to act with the humility of the mason who paves the roads. The man who paves the roads works with his toil and sweat; he knows that for decades after he has finished paving the road, millions of people will travel on those roads. They will travel with hope in their heart and ambition in their eyes, trying to seek out a fortune for themselves in whatever they are doing; but not once will they ever stop to think about the man who paved the road for them. A business leader must be like the mason—an anonymous servant of those travellers. But being an anonymous servant of humanity is very much a part of a leader's privilege, and not his plight.

When that idea seizes leaders, the concept of trusteeship leaps out at them. It makes leadership effulgent and meaningful. When you depart from this world, it is not your name or fame but what you leave behind that can make the biggest difference to someone.

THE CURSE OF THE SUPERSTAR CEO

Equally important is the role of the CEO. Capitalism and modern media have made the CEO the hero of the company. But you have to ask yourself a question: does the CEO really do all this by himself? Is the portrayal of the CEO in this manner realistic? It is but human that when you see your picture on the cover of a magazine and your name being flashed all over; you start to believe that you are the cause of the company's success. After all, we are all gods of clay and we fall into that trap.

A story from the Bhagavata Purana reinforces this fact. The Yadava clan, to which Lord Krishna belonged, had been cursed that someday, they would die by self-destruction.

After the great war of Kurukshetra (recounted in the Mahabharata), the Yadavas, under the leadership of Lord Krishna, went to Dwarka, which is not far from Mithapur where Tata Chemicals now runs a factory.

In Dwarka, the Yadavas started slaughtering each other as the curse took effect. Therefore, Lord Krishna sent a message to Yudhishthira in Indraprastha, requesting that the valiant Arjuna be sent forthwith. It was believed that only Arjuna could save the situation and prevent the Yadavas from annihilating each other. So, Arjuna came riding on his chariot all the way to Dwarka from Indraprastha and found that there was bedlam. He decided that the only way to save the clan was to rescue the Yadava women. That way the clan could continue. So he assembled as many Yadava women as he could on his convoy, and rode out of Dwarka.

On his way back to Indraprastha, Arjuna felt elated with his performance, a bit like the modern-day CEO. As he went through the countryside, dasyus (a native community) attacked the convoy. The very valiant Arjuna tried to save the women. He drew his time-tested and magical bow and arrow; but for some reason, it didn't work this time. The great hero of many wars, the indefatigable Arjuna, could not overpower the dasyus. The poet Tulsidas wrote the following evocative lines on the encounter:

Tulsi narse kyaa badaa, samay badaa balwaan
Kaaravan looti gopikaa, wohi arjun wohi baan

(Tulsidas says that of the greatness of a man, time is the great arbiter. When the caravan was being looted of the women, the same Arjun with the same fighting implements could not overcome them.)

This is what happens to CEO's around the world. People who are treated as great heroes today are often treated as zeros tomorrow.

The role of the CEO is to be the ultimate servant of society. It is not just his efforts, but the sweat and labour of the many hundreds of thousands working in a company that is behind the company's success. The leader's job is to communicate with them. But it takes a superhero to actually downplay his own role and promote the idea that he happens to be the trustee of the efforts of all the people who work for him and help the company to do so well.

THE NIRVANA OF BUSINESS

During my time at the Tatas, I used to visit various units in remote locations—a fertilizer factory in Uttar Pradesh (UP), a hydroelectric plant in the Western Ghats or a chemical plant in Gujarat. Almost always, the presentations began in the way that presentations were made to me during my earlier career: what are the challenges that the management faces and how is it overcoming them? The unstated message being that the team was right on top of its job and the company's interest was in safe hands. But what struck me was that the presentations always ended in a unique way. What were they doing with the community around them?

It really didn't matter whether there were six people in a hydroelectric power station or sixty managers in a fertilizer factory or 6000 managers in a large steel factory. There was always concern for the community around us. To be honest, I was initially a bit sceptical. When you have reached your early fifties, you tend to become a bit cynical about what might appear to be a public relations put-on.

By the time I visited many units, it became clear that it could not be a put-on. I have never come across a circular from Bombay House which tells managers that their presentation must end that way. People just do it because they are genuinely of the view that their job is to earn profit for the betterment of the community. It is to the community that they must return what they earn. There cannot be a better commentary on trusteeship than when people actually act and behave in that manner instead of just making presentations; when people believe in it and don't have to make an effort to do so; when it is not a programmed thing; when they practise trusteeship because it is the very reason why they are there. Such a situation is the nirvana of business—it would earn business a respectful place in society, and business people can hold their head high.

DOING IT THE TATA WAY

One of the notable things about Tata is the shareholding pattern. It allows Tata to do the right things in the right way, with an eye on the long-term. Tata companies are promoted by a company called Tata Sons, a private and unlisted company. Thus the parent company is unlisted, while the subsidiary companies are listed—such as Tata Steel, Tata Consultancy, Tata Motors, Tata Chemicals, Tata Power and so on.

There are close to three million shareholders of the son-companies, the grandson-companies, and the great grandson-companies. The principal shareholder of the parent holding company, Tata Sons, is a clutch of charitable trusts which is worth billions of dollars. Therefore, I think that this structure embeds certain values which if you do not practise, you do not belong. It gives you a sense of humility and humanity, whereby you can run the company and yet try to be a servant of society. If that can be imparted and translated across as many Tata companies as we have, it will be quite significant. I used to go to work every morning, fighting to get every single extra rupee or dollar of profit to the extent of my influence or position. There were 700,000 other people doing the same thing. We do this because a significant portion of the extra dollar goes to charity. When we hopefully go to Vaikuntha after leaving this world, we may have something to say for ourselves—and that thought is a big help!

I wish all businesses could adopt one of these trusteeship models. Tata is trying to spread these ideas to companies that they acquire around the world, and these companies are completely electrified and captivated. I have discussed this concept of trusteeship and the way Tata has practised it with the managers of our acquired companies in Detroit, Northwich, UK and Singapore: they just don't believe that this is possible. Gradually the penny drops and they realize that only a very rare and unique kind of organization could actually do this.

I would hope that in the course of time, it will make people believe that business can be humane and need not be an inhuman pursuit of greed.

4

Flying Once More Across the Sky

During a visit to China in early 2016, I learnt of how Chinese labour had been ravaged because of the ongoing industrial restructuring in the Guangdong province. Older factories were closing, workers were being laid off, and new factories were coming up. There was considerable disquiet among the working class. The policy of the Guangdong government was reported to be *Thong Long Huan Niao*, a Cantonese expression that means 'Open the cage and let the birds fly.' As I understood it, the provincial government likened the uncompetitive companies to caged birds and encouraged them to fly out and design a new life for themselves and their workers.

To draw an analogy, the Indian industry was in a similar situation in 1991 when liberalization occurred. The bird cages were indeed opened with the tectonic changes to

Insurance Regulatory and Development Authority (IDRA), Monopolistic and Restrictive Trade Practise (MRTP) Act and Foreign Exchange Regulation Act (FERA)—three key laws which held industry on a draconian leash. Industrial licensing, monopoly laws and foreign exchange transactions were relaxed, diluted and modified over a period of time.

During this momentous period of contemporary economic history, it would be interesting to understand the dilemmas, transformations and the pathway out of the 'cage' of two companies—Hindustan Unilever Ltd (HUL, but referred to as HLL) and Tata (as a group of companies).

THE CHILDREN OF LIBERALIZATION, AS I SAW THEM

The events of liberalization are viewed differently by different players, depending on where they observed it and experienced its developments from. As far as I am concerned, in January 1991, some months before the liberalization, I moved to Jeddah as Chairman, Unilever Arabia. Things were not going well in India at that time; for that matter, nor was Arabia very inviting, what with clouds over Kuwait followed by the Gulf War. I was apprehensive about how events would unfold in both geographies.

Within a few months, unexpected by me, there were dramatic developments in India, which I watched from Jeddah. At the end of 1994, I returned as Managing Director of Brooke Bond Lipton India Ltd. and, thereafter, as Vice Chairman of Hindustan Lever. Through these roles, I personally experienced the maelstrom of liberalization. As part of the team with HLL Chairman Susim Datta and colleagues, I participated in a dramatic rearrangement of the Unilever businesses in India. Some years later, I joined Tata Sons as a Director, and as part of the team with Ratan Tata and colleagues, I participated in the rearrangement of the Tata Group. Both of these have been hugely impactful experiences from a professional point of view.

So what transpired out there in the companies as liberalization occurred? What new degrees of freedom did they get out of this historic decision? Finally, what were some of their dilemmas and how were they resolved? The answers to these critical questions can be better understood through a few events that I witnessed first-hand, or could relate with closely.

HLL and Tata are two-storied business groups with a couple of centuries of existence between them; they responded to this new era and renewed themselves as the 'children of liberalization'. HLL was very keen on expanding in the Indian market, while Tata was eager to expand both in the domestic and into the international markets. HLL was (and is) the 'most Indian multinational' company, and Tata, the 'most multinational Indian' group.

As an aside, I will also very briefly touch upon the wave of start-ups. I will highlight the rise of a non-technology Indian company, Patanjali Ayurved Limited, which has rapidly built a somewhat controversial FMCG business of a size that took Unilever a century to build. Patanjali would not have happened without liberalization.

I have tried to interweave the stories to some degree, especially where there are points of overlap.

THE EARLY YEARS

HLL and the levers of success

In 1990, when Susim Datta became Chairman of HLL, he inherited a fairly strong company, which had weathered numerous challenges in the infamous license-permit-quota raj. The vexatious issue of 51 per cent foreign equity for Unilever under FERA had lasted through the 1970s and 1980s. It finally got resolved through the strenuous efforts of T. Thomas and Ashok Ganguly, two earlier chairmen. HLL, being a FERA company, was not allowed to increase production of detergents or source from third-parties. Therefore, the company had not been able to respond effectively to the market threat posed by Nirma, a small-scale manufacturer of detergents. Even before liberalization, in the early 1980s, HLL grabbed the invitation of the Punjab government to buy into the equity of a sick, government-owned detergent company, Stepan Chemicals. Being outside the ambit of FERA, Stepan Chemicals was permitted to outsource products from third parties. What a circuitous route to take to get production capacity! To conform to FERA, HLL had entered into the chemicals and exports businesses, both of which had reasonably stabilized. But if there was to be liberalization of some sort, these just-stabilized businesses would face fresh challenges.

The winds of change had been blowing through government and administrative corridors since the early 1980s, but they could not develop into a strong gale because of several political developments. As Datta reflected on the contemporary national developments, it became obvious that dramatic change was around the corner. The trouble was that nobody knew what exactly the change would be and how dramatic it would be. For many decades, multinational company leaders had been advocating for a liberal free-market and consumer-driven markets as a panacea for India's development. Their advocacy flowered into a reality quite suddenly in May 1991, when Prime Minister P.V. Narasimha Rao (industry portfolio), Dr Manmohan Singh (finance portfolio), and P. Chidambaram (commerce portfolio) embarked on liberalizing industry and trade. HLL was psychologically prepared for change, but not in any specific form, because the contours of the change were not known.

In the initial period after liberalization, the company decided to seek external advice and engaged Prof. Sumantra Ghoshal of London Business School to work with the leadership team. It would have been difficult to get foreign exchange approval for such consultancy during the license raj era. Liberalization appeared to bring with it new uncertainties, so HLL developed alternative scenarios along with an aggressive vision: to double sales every four years and double profits-after-tax every three years. This was akin to a pilot deciding to break the sound barrier with no prior experience of the resultant sonic boom—the pace of the company would have to increase to a level that nobody had experienced before. Such thinking became possible entirely due to liberalization.

Now HLL could expand production capacity and set up new capacities without the painful process of applying to the government for industrial licenses. Even before 1991, HLL had built a couple of new factories, thanks to a government policy for industrially backward areas of the country. However, it could not refresh or resize its existing factories. Within the first decade-and-a-half of liberalization, none of the six factories that produced commodities when I joined the company (Bombay, Garden Reach, Shamnagar, Ghaziabad, Trichy, and Etah) remained in a recognizable form. Most were sold or closed down due to labour issues, product obsolescence or uncompetitive cost structures. Brand new and modern factories with new work practises were put up. Such a renewal of manufacturing could just not have been contemplated, let alone executed, during the license-permit days. Datta later recounted, 'I would like to believe that although the initial problems were very large, in the end this dispersal of the manufacturing facilities has helped the company—certainly it did during the years I was there. It was against this backdrop that HLL settled into a period of growth, an era of mergers and acquisitions, and a period when there was a lot of media attention on us.'

HLL developed an enormous appetite for organic growth, something that industrial licensing had thwarted for all these years. This aspect of the company did not fetch newspaper headlines, but some of the biggest successes were achieved through organic growth. The company's large detergents division led the charge, by developing the vision, foresight and courage to improve its market presence by adopting a target of making and marketing '1 million tonnes by 1994'. Before liberalization, HLL's detergent division was selling about 450,000 tonnes and this new ambition and the drive to get the growth to reach a million tonnes by 1994 was perceived as big, audacious and gutsy. HLL achieved this growth through organic means by building completely new factories and by backing chosen brands, which included Wheel detergent bar.

Another aspect that HLL had to completely reorient was consumer research. The company already had strong skills in market research, but realized that those would not be adequate to meet the needs of the future. Due to global exposure through media, the consumer would change rapidly, his expectations would escalate sharply, and competition would aggressively track these developments. The expenditure on consumer research was upped progressively and new techniques like Simulated Test Markets, Sequential Recycling and Qualitative Research were implemented.

Tradition meets modernity at Tata

Just a kilometre away from the HLL office, a newly appointed corporate leader sat in his fourth floor office at the eponymous Bombay House. On 23 March 1991, patriarch J.R.D. Tata had his 'usual' Monday morning meeting with his acolyte, Ratan Tata. However, the patriarch said something unusual at this usual meeting, 'I have decided to retire as chairman and to appoint you in my place as Chairman of Tata Sons… I have not decided the date because I have to consult Ajit Kerkar.' Ajit Kerkar, the Chairman of Indian Hotels, was very good at picking auspicious dates and J.R.D. clearly wanted the day to be an auspicious one. A wonderful example of tradition woven into modernity!

After the initial period of what Ratan Tata subsequently termed 'basking in the glory of the change', he settled down to the task of thinking about what his agenda should be. In reality, Ratan Tata had started thinking about transforming the group's operations a decade earlier, when the redoubtable J.R.D. Tata had appointed him as the Chairman of Tata Industries. In that capacity, Ratan Tata had scripted a 'Corporate Plan', a sort of blueprint for the group, with some assumptions about the economy and government policy. The plan had to wait several years for the mantle of leadership to fall on his shoulders—and so, coincidentally, the magic of liberalization.

Like many other companies, Tata companies, in particular the flagship Tata Steel and Tata Motors, had suffered for decades during the licence raj era with its unjustifiable controls over production and pricing, mindless quotas for allocation of resources and severe restrictions on imports. Foreign exchange controls meant that companies had to struggle to persuade officials while importing new machinery or deploying state-of-the-art technology; even business leaders and top executives found it difficult to travel abroad on business trips as there was a ceiling on the amount of foreign exchange that could be spent on a per diem basis.

A company like Tata Motors, for instance, had a licence to manufacture just 50,000 commercial vehicles per year in the mid-1970s. The average cost of a truck was ₹100,000 per vehicle, and the profit margin was a mere ₹4,000 on each vehicle. There was an underdeveloped vendor base and the company had to produce everything that went into a truck. In that era of scarcity, it was virtually impossible to import anything; yet, certain critical items had to be bought abroad—for instance, pens (and ink) to make blueprints. It cost a whopping ₹3,500 to import a single drawing pen, equivalent to the profit from a whole truck.

The odds were loaded heavily against the Tata group. It was a relatively small Indian business entity in a world dominated by giants with deep pockets; it lacked scale, and operated mainly in just one market, India, when its international rivals had the advantage of operations across the globe. It was involved in a bewildering assortment of industries, and lacked focus, thanks to the restrictive laws. Most of its revenues and profits were derived from commodity businesses; its own few brands were weak compared with global brands.

Bound by an older, slower style of functioning, the Tata group had considerable work ahead to face the fast-paced competition of the future. It was concerned about quality, but given the lack of customer orientation—a mark of the protected Indian industry in general—it had to do a lot more to match market-savvy rivals. And quality had yet to pervade all aspects of operations and strategizing.

Ratan Tata started a series of dinner meetings with his acquaintances at McKinsey. Through these discussions, he came to the conclusion that the group should be restructured to become more competitive, to provide better returns to the shareholders, to be more nimble-footed or more proactive to the changing scene than it had been in the past. These meetings led to the articulation of a set of papers for discussion with the Tata Sons board. The plan was to critically look at the many Tata companies through a group mechanism which did not exist up until that point of time. It should be mentioned that the MRTP regulations imposed burdens on the group concept.

It was thus that the Group Executive Office (GEO) was born, which I joined from my perch as Vice Chairman of

HLL. The intention was that the GEO would consist of a group of executive directors of Tata Sons who would have the responsibility of overseeing the performance of various operating companies. The GEO would also look critically at restructuring the group by way of mergers, acquisitions of our core businesses, as well as divestments of companies that were in businesses which were not considered core, or where the Tata market position was not predominant. Several of these ideas and concepts could be considered only because of liberalization in the business environment.

Following the establishment of the GEO, the group devised three more 'welding' mechanisms, which included the setting up of a common, unified brand, an explicit code of conduct (which had been implicit earlier as well) and a set of operating requirements for companies that used the brand.

Ratan Tata's first hard decision was on the Tata Oil Mills Company (TOMCO), which had built a detergents and soaps business for the group since 1923. The Tata group identified the core sectors to concentrate on and grow. TOMCO had been losing money for some years and it appeared as though the business would not fit into the Tata view of its future. Soaps and detergents were, on the other hand, core to HLL. It was, therefore, an opportune moment for the two companies to ink a mutually beneficial agreement. The Tata decision to exit TOMCO and the HLL appetite to acquire it for growth went through the appropriate processes. TOMCO was acquired and merged into HLL.

The TOMCO sale was a dramatic development, unimaginable just a few years previously in the India of old. Not surprisingly, it emerged as the most newsworthy and sizeable acquisition of the time. There were difficulties galore: the regulatory formalities, getting the proposals passed through the respective boards, and resolving the legal aspects of the merger. It was a crucial turn in the HLL growth story, and just as crucial a step in the Tata divestment approach. Ratan Tata faced so much criticism from within the group that, as he confessed later, he became hesitant to undertake further divestments. TOMCO's managers received the HLL integration team with considerable suspicion, though the two learned to work collaboratively to consummate the deal. The HLL integration team was delighted when Ratan Tata expressed his appreciation of how the team handled the acquisition.

HRD on the transformation agenda

To better appreciate the constraints under which companies operated prior to liberalization, it is important to examine two key factors of production—people and capital.

The remuneration paid to directors of companies used to be controlled by the Companies Act. Even if a company was making reasonable profits, the managerial remuneration was restricted by Company Law. Throughout the license permit raj, there had been significant brain drain from India because top-qualified professionals sought greener pastures in overseas markets in search of better remuneration. After liberalization, the pernicious ceiling on remuneration was significantly relaxed. Profit-making companies could pay their top talent, using principles of meritocracy, market rates and affordability. The scenario changed the talent market dramatically. Over a period of time, professional talent in India could earn and save pretty much what was possible in other countries. Thus, the managerial talent market also got liberalized by the events of 1991.

HLL stepped up the globalization of its managers by seconding about 1000 managers abroad over the next quarter century. At any point of time, one hundred HLL managers were on overseas secondment into jobs within Unilever. In this way, a large pool of managers with a global mind-set was trained. Many continued within Unilever and HLL, but, in due course, several found leadership roles in other companies in Indian industry.

Tata also placed human resource development on its transformation agenda when its work with McKinsey was ready for implementation. Tata Consultancy Services (TCS), for example, had to design and implement HR systems for the tens of thousands of knowledge workers it was recruiting each year. In the new century, TCS was recruiting 5,000 to 6,000 technically qualified engineers per month—and training them to deal, with a global mind-set, with customers who were largely overseas!

A Boost to corporate governance

With regard to equity capital, the office of the Controller of Capital Issues got abolished. Companies could now test the market to price their fresh equity on a market-based approach. This required improved corporate governance. The appointment of a hugely talented civil servant, G.V. Ramakrishna, as Chairman of the Securities and Exchange Board of India (SEBI) brought in new regulations, which allowed new degrees of responsible freedom to well-intentioned companies. Indian entrepreneurs developed very fast into the new growth areas like software, telecom and infrastructure. Meaningful and successful IPOs like Infosys, TCS, Biocon and Bharti Telecom would have been impossible to build under the earlier regime of the Controller of Capital Issues. The league table of the Top 100 companies witnessed a big churn in the rankings through the entry and exit of players.

THE LATER YEARS

HLL on a mergers and acquisitions spree

Apart from pushing for organic growth and an early acquisition of TOMCO, HLL refocused its thrust on several vectors. First was a major product quality drive by benchmarking locally produced products with imports, pointing to the urgent need for upgradation. HLL internally proselytized techniques like Total Productivity Maintenance (TPM), and considered imports of machines and packaging materials as required. Second was the special emphasis on product innovation and the setting-up of a second international R&D centre at Bangalore. Third was extended, multifarious business collaborations with the parent Unilever. Earlier, Unilever could not be remitted brand, technical or service fees, but such expenses could now be paid under the new dispensation.

After acquiring TOMCO, there were many more high profile mergers and acquisitions (M&A) activities. HLL went on to acquire Lakme from Tata (after appropriate governance processes were done on both sides, which goes without saying). HLL also divested its phosphate chemicals business to Tata Chemicals. The acquisition of the public sector company Modern Bakeries from the government followed. Later, HLL divested its hair oil brand, Nihar, and purchased an Ayurvedic hair oil brand called Indulekha.

Being a global leader in ice creams, Unilever had, for long, been very keen on establishing an ice cream business in India. Under the license-permit raj, dairy ice cream was reserved for small-scale manufacture, being one out of some 750 items so reserved. On the grounds that vegetable fat-based products, which were called frozen desserts by HLL, were different from dairy ice cream, Brooke Bond Lipton set up a brand new investment at Nashik and launched Walls Frozen Desserts. This became very controversial at that time, though the controversy died a natural death with subsequent de-reservation of several reservations, including ice cream.

Cadbury's ice cream operations were acquired by Brooke Bond Lipton. The company entered into a hugely complex deal to acquire four independent Kwality ice cream entities, all of which used a common brand name. This could help Unilever establish an ice cream business in India. The Kissan tomato products business was acquired from the flamboyant Vijay Mallya, as also the Zahura tomato plant from PepsiCo India. It was an appropriate vehicle for the ambitious plans that Brooke Bond's foods business had for the branded products market.

As the Managing Director of Brooke Bond Lipton, I found that the employees had experienced as many as ten mergers within just the previous four years: first Brooke Bond acquired Lipton, then Doom Dooma Assam and Tea Estates India, followed by Kissan, Milkfoods, Zahura and four differently-owned Kwality entities. As an aside, I might point out that the resultant company suffered from a considerable bout of indigestion. In a quandary about how to handle management morale, I casually asked an assistant hailing from Kerala what the future bore for the company. Being a trained astrologer, he promptly cast the company horoscope after ascertaining the date of birth from the company's registration certificate and pronounced, 'This company has so far behaved as a man, and has given the company's name to several people he has married. The company will get peace of mind by behaving like a woman, and by taking the name of the husband she should marry.' His astrological opinion did not at all influence the subsequent decision to merge Brooke Bond Lipton into Hindustan Lever. It became the biggest merger and was also highly controversial because it led to some legal cases.

The winds of liberalization brought in global ideas into business. But in the case of HLL, this began in the mid-1980s, slightly ahead of liberalization. HLL strived to be productive, not only in economic terms, but also in terms of benefitting the environment. HLL started its first experiment in this regard with Chhindwara in Madhya Pradesh, where it began to recycle significant quantities of treated effluent back into the manufacturing process or on land for irrigation. This saved costs for the company and ensured that HLL's operations would not strain the rural environment. The chemical engineers in the factories explored the possibility of designing zero effluent factories long before it became a part of sustainability programmes. Re-forestation attempts at Khamgaon in Maharashtra were started for similar reasons.

In 1991, HLL earned revenues of $700 million, which have grown to about $10 billion now. The company's market capitalization has grown from $900 million to over $50 billion currently.

The non-Tata way of solving problems

The Tata group seized the opportunities presented by the reforms and embarked on a remarkable journey that has, over the past quarter century, transformed it into a vibrant and global business house.

With MRTP gone, Ratan Tata increased the group ownership in the major companies and re-established Tata Sons as the focal point of the group, an opposite action to what J.R.D. Tata had done earlier to comply with the MRTP legislation. Where increase of shareholding was not possible, as in the case of Associated Cement Company (ACC), Tata shareholding was sold to an international cement major. Some group companies like Forbes, Campbell and Tata Infomedia were divested from Tata. There were multiple companies in the same market space and, over time, attempts were made to rationalize them; for example, Tata Steel's power plants were bought by Tata Power. Tata Infotech, and the public sector company, CMC, were both acquired by TCS at different points of time and later were merged into TCS in separate public transactions.

The serial mention of these moves does not mean that the decisions were easily accepted or implemented through a command and control mechanism. Each one required a de novo debate with directors of different boards; each one was perceived at the time to be a 'non-Tata way' of solving a problem, and there followed a sequence of cajoling, determination and doggedness while implementing them.

Several Tata companies also had their heads buried in the sand. Many businesses looked inwards and measured themselves against their own past performance. The external impression was that Tata was less nimble than others, more resistant to change and extremely fixed in its ways. Unless Tata companies were bench-marked against the brightest and the best, the probability of change was going to be low. In the early years, Ratan Tata observed candidly, 'We have yet to seek excellence in all that we do. We hang a picture slightly crooked and live with it for ten years; this should bother us the first time we see it, and keep on bothering us until it is set right.'

The Tata group adopted the Tata Business Excellence Model (TBEM), based on the quality improvement framework developed for the Malcolm Baldrige National Quality Awards (MBNQA), first launched in the US as a means of responding to the quality challenge presented by Japan Inc. in the 1980s. In February 1995, the first batch of assessors met at the Tata Management Training Centre (TMTC) for in-depth training on the Baldrige model. They assessed twelve Tata companies, and the average score was an abysmal 215 out of a maximum score of 1,000 (nowadays, all the major Tata companies have crossed 500, while several have passed 600). The alarm bells rang, loud and clear. The journey was to be long, painful and exhausting, but liberalization demanded that Tata undertake the journey, even if only for survival.

The first winner of the JRD Quality Value Award for performance within the TBEM framework was Tata Steel in 2000. It went on to win the Deming Prize in 2008, and then the coveted Grand Deming Prize in 2012. Indeed, TBEM set the tone and created the foundation for a critical transformational exercise in the group. It has also been the glue in binding the group together and enhancing the Tata brand.

The opening up of the economy, the removal of unnecessary restrictions relating to investments and the relaxation in foreign exchange rules emboldened the Tata group to break out of its traditional orbit and head for other geographies. This created capabilities within Tata companies to compete successfully in the Indian market, and thereafter grow in international markets with the confidence of being able to hold their own against their global peers.

DOING DISAGREEABLE THINGS IN AN AGREEABLE WAY

There were many group company events and anecdotes that related closely to liberalization, but four are particularly worth mentioning. The first is the dramatic restructuring undertaken by Tata Steel during the 1990s. Within a decade, Tata Steel had been transformed by downsizing the workforce to about half its starting size. The remarkable thing was that this tough decision was implemented with empathy and humaneness; the Tata action became symbolic of how to do disagreeable things in an agreeable way. The plants were modernized with new technologies and a management mindset was instilled, one which could dream and execute big transformations. The second event is the entry of Tata Motors into the passenger car business. During the earlier stewardship of J.R.D. Tata and Sumant Moolgaokar in the 1970s, truck maker TELCO, as it was then known, was denied an industrial license to manufacture passenger cars in a new joint venture (JV) with Honda. When Ratan Tata took over as chairman of Tata Motors, he proposed something daring: to design and launch an indigenous passenger car, ground up. Tata Indica was launched in 1999, and later, the Tata Nano. Irrespective of the market reception or performance of these products, even a critic or cynic would concede that both events were transformative not only for Tata, but for all of India Inc.

The third is the difficult decision by Tata Sons to press ahead with a TCS Initial Public Offering (IPO). By the mid-1990s, TCS cash flows had become material through the Y2K boom. TCS evolved the practise of retaining half its profit with the balance being used by Tata Sons. This was a huge benefit to Tata Sons as they were able to use the TCS export revenues to reduce the tax exposure on the dividend income. Further, an aggressive TCS, ranked beyond 30th among global IT players in 2000, set itself the difficult goal of breaking into the top 10 globally, not just in terms of revenue but also profitability and other transparently stated metrics. The company had worked with Professor Pankaj Ghemawat but, in a sense, had stumbled onto this audacious goal through its internal brain-storming. The company set about its task through a huge organizational transformation to help its people think globally about customers, work processes and quality. On 25 August, 2004, as the success of the TCS IPO became clear—easily becoming India's largest and most complex IPO—there was jubilation within Tata and a new aspiration for Indian business houses in general.

While all these three events are positive stories for liberalization, the fourth event concerning the airlines business, did not have a happy ending. As the parent of Air India before the iconic company was nationalized, Tata always harboured a deep desire to re-enter the airline business. When airline entry rules were liberalized in the 1990s, Tata spent considerable effort to execute a business plan through a joint venture (JV) with Singapore Airlines. After a great deal of advocacy and diligence, Tata's efforts were frustrated and the company unhappily withdrew its application. It was a painful reminder that crony capitalism was still alive and kicking in a rapidly liberalizing India.

BUILDING BRAND INDIA ACROSS THE GLOBE

The adherence of Tata companies to both the TBEM process and the Tata Code of Conduct was permanently enshrined in the Brand Equity and Business Promotion (BEBP) Agreement. Each Tata company subscribed to this agreement in order to secure the right to use the Tata brand. This played an immense role in presenting to the world Tata products and services that stand for performance and trust. Alongside key initiatives in governance, brand promotion and business excellence, the Tata group quickly developed an understanding of the critical importance of innovation in order to successfully compete in the global economy.

This eventually led to the formation of the Tata Group Innovation Forum in 2007, and the celebration of the group's pioneering instincts through annual Tata Innovista Awards. The group's recent disclosure of having crossed a milestone of 7,000 patent applications, a number that has doubled in just the last two years, reflects the rapid progress that the group is making.

Twenty-five years ago, the Tata group had a turnover of just $6 billion. By 2017-18, group revenues topped $140 billion. Back then, Tata had little by way of overseas operations; today, it operates in more than a hundred countries across the globe. Beginning with Tata Tea's acquisition of Tetley in 2000, the group made several significant overseas acquisitions, including Corus by Tata Steel, Jaguar and Land Rover by Tata Motors and Brunner Mond by Tata Chemicals—all in the UK; Daewoo Commercial Vehicles by Tata Motors in South Korea; NatSteel in Singapore and Millennium Steel in Thailand by Tata Steel; and General Chemical Industrial

Products by Tata Chemicals, Eight O' Clock Coffee by Tata Tea and Tyco Global Network by Tata Communications in the US. In 2014–15, the group had international revenues of $73 billion, accounting for 67 per cent of total revenues. The twenty-nine publicly-listed Tata enterprises had a combined market capitalisation of about $150 billion by 2018.

Though the unshackling of the Indian economy led to dramatic changes within the group, its core ethos and emphasis on ethical business practises and its commitment to the communities in which it operates have not changed. The journey since the reforms process began has been exciting for the Tata group, which has rejuvenated existing businesses, entered new ones, aggressively expanded in the overseas markets and launched breakthrough products. Today, the companies in the Tata group are building brand India all across the globe. The lofty and refreshed vision for the Tata group is that by 2025, 25 per cent of the world's population should experience the Tata commitment to improving the quality of life of customers and communities.

NEW POSTER BOYS OF GROWTH

Yet another phenomenon that is a derivative of liberalization is the arrival of a bunch of new messiahs, born and nurtured in the post-liberalization atmosphere. These were IT driven start-up businesses, helped along by the development of a supporting ecosystem. These ventures were based on disintermediating traditional business models, and became possible because institutions like venture funding and entrepreneurship mentoring also entered the business space.

Interestingly, a non-technology-based start-up called Patanjali also took birth and is reported to have grown rapidly. In 1993, a twenty-five-year-old youth named Ramkrishna Yadav established a flourishing yoga practise and soon became famous as Baba Ramdev. Nobody could have imagined that this rustic youth would build a commercially competitive FMCG entity within ten years, to the same size which HLL took a century to achieve! He owned three to four yoga and spirituality television channels, which are reported to have developed a viewership of about 200 million. Prior to liberalization, a private party could not have owned a television channel.

His story gains some importance in the context of this narrative because even as century-old companies like HLL and Tata were adapting to modernity and open markets, Baba Ramdev began a process of modernizing the 3,000 year old tradition of yoga. Charak, Zandu, Dabur, Vicco Vajradanti, Kesh King, Chandrika, Himalaya and many more had been around for decades. However, the newest wellness brand, Patanjali, attracted consumer interest and franchise to a far stronger degree than any of the predecessor brands. The views and reasons for its apparently instantaneous success range from good brand stewardship, supply chain/marketing savvy and intuitive play on a latent consumer longing for 'natural' products on one end, to a less complimentary view—that it is a form of politically-inspired crony capitalism. It all depends on who you speak to! The fact is that such an endeavour could not have happened without liberalization. Prior to liberalization, every new entrepreneur would have had to get his unit classified as a 'small scale unit' or, if a large industrial undertaking, obtain an industrial license to set up his unit. The access to foreign exchange for import of process or packing machines was painful. The entrepreneur would have had to spend considerable time 'cultivating' the numerous inspectors and authorities to keep his unit functioning. No dramatic market impact could be planned until many years of painstaking effort had been expended. None of these are necessary any longer.

Start-ups promise to be the new poster boys of growth; though the outlook is ambiguous and is constantly debated, start-ups, digital or otherwise, are also the children of liberalization.

WHEN INDIA AVERTED A CONVERSATION WITH DEATH

We can consider the fitness and business performance of Indian companies in the before-liberalization (BL) and after-liberalization (AL) eras. Evolution teaches us that the longest-surviving species are not the biggest, the fastest or the strongest, but the most adaptive ones. HLL-AL is still India's top FMCG Company, but the company is very different from the HLL-BL, just like Tata. Yet both companies have many more tasks ahead.

Five data points over the last seventy-five years, dating back to when the lists of top business groups were published by public authorities, speak for themselves. In 1939, the *Indian Business and Nationalist Politics* published that Tata was India's number 1 group; it was so again in 1951 (*RK Hazari Report on the Corporate Private Sector*), and it continued to be so in 1969 (*Licensing Policy Enquiry Committee*), 1990 (Gita Piramal, *Big Business and Entrepreneurship*), and 2016 (*Capitaline Database*).

To become number one is not easy. To stay number one for seventy-five years is incredibly tough. This is a small measure of corporate adaptiveness, especially when, during the same period, the half-life of Fortune 500 companies has rapidly declined.

The years of protection and the consequent lack of competitiveness of Indian industry in 1991 is emotively captured by a Paulo Coelho blog from 10 November 2010, 'The Bird and the Cage'.[1] A woman loved a bird so much that she caged the bird. After captivity, the bird gradually withered away and died. The woman felt miserable and started to wither away herself. One day, she had a visitation from Death. 'Why have you come?' she asked Death. 'So that you can fly once more with the bird across the sky,'

---

[1] http://paulocoelhoblog.com/2010/11/10/the-bird-and-the-cage/

Death replied. At the risk of dramatizing the situation, Indian companies were the caged bird and the Indian economy was the woman. Thankfully, India averted such a conversation with Death.

5

The #EtTu Movement in India Inc.

All things change; nothing abides,
Into the same river, one cannot step twice.
—HERACLITUS

Agility and adaptability are buzzwords that define a company not only through periods of policy change and reform but also during the twists and turns of a leadership transition. Though there is considerable management writing as well as research on leadership succession planning, nothing much is known about predecessor planning. They are, I think, two halves of the same fruit. It takes thought and introspection to be and to behave like a good predecessor.

Those days are fast disappearing when CEOs could enjoy

an affectionate retirement function, have their wonderful qualities and accomplishments enumerated, and continue some sort of an association with their beloved company—maybe as an advisor or non-executive director. Fifty years ago, it looked as though the good life could just carry on, but not anymore.

Why #EtTu? *Et tu, Brute* is a Latin phrase immortalized by William Shakespeare in his play, *Julius Caesar*, in which those words were uttered by the Roman dictator Julius Caesar to Brutus at the time of the former's assassination—'You too, Brutus?'

I often wonder if an #EtTu movement is developing in the business world. Increasingly, investors and stakeholders desire that a successor deploy a fresh point of view to solve persistent issues—as would currently be expected from the CEOs of Infosys or Axis Bank. In fact, the track record of past CEOs could well be reopened and re-evaluated. I see signs of that movement in many companies, if not all, to reconsider and set right past decisions. This causes great angst among employees and observers—the predecessor or past CEO probably enjoys a halo, and is surely perceived to have done many great things, having retired with a God-like reputation—and now his or her past actions from several years ago are being reviewed in hindsight! Think of what is happening to Jack Welch (General Electric/GE) now, or Percy Barnevik (ABB), or what happened to Richard Wagoner (General Motors/GM) several years ago.

In #EtTu, investors want the successor to examine the blunders made during the tenure of the preceeding CEO, and make post facto judgements for action. This is not to write history; investors desire that the incoming CEO recognize the weaknesses and correct them at the earliest. Such an analysis and debate does not suit the 'bhakts' of the predecessor. For sure, there could be many frayed nerves. Such a review can spoil the predecessor's peace of mind. Regulators, investors, analysts and employees may criticize the past leader's tenure, sometimes castigate past leadership or, in extreme cases involving public matters, even bring the past leader to a court trial. A retired leader runs the risk of facing an #EtTu moment in the evening of his or her career, based on how events pan out and how successors view the past in current times.

For example, a seventy-year-old telecommunications IAS officer was pulled out of retirement to answer for decisions taken during his tenure over a decade earlier. So, too, was an IAS officer who worked as a coal mining administrator. A former bank chairman's decisions were reviewed after a decade, because some loans that were given during his tenure went sour later. These being public subjects involving government officers, such incidents had a strong dollop of politics driving the actions.

There are instructive company examples in the private sector too. First, a case from my old company, Unilever. Just like Roger Federer and Novak Djokovic partnered in tennis doubles for Team Europe in 2018 and became the only European pair to *lose* the match, similarly, during the 1990s, Unilever had two competent and talented joint chairmen, heading the British and the Dutch subsidiaries. Individually, they were arguably the brightest chairmen ever. Yet this combination of two exceptional leaders produced substandard results for Unilever, causing a drastic restructuring of the way the company had been run for several decades. Things have worked out well for Unilever since then.

From 1998 till 2005, the Indian subsidiary of Unilever went through a rough patch, causing public reports and commentaries discussing whether a mess had been left for successors to clean up. The continuing leadership turmoil at P&G has provoked commentaries on the decisions and actions of previous CEOs and the legacy they left for their successors.

At GE, contemporary commentators hearken back to the fabled Jack Welch years to judge the legacies of inheritance and management. Writing in the *Financial Times*[1], John Gapper expressed his view, 'John Flannery was handed the job of catching the falling knives from Mr Immelt's era… GE is so fragile after nearly four decades of asset shuffling under Mr Immelt and his predecessor Jack Welch…'

In the emerging #EtTu movement in the corporate world,

---

[1] John Gapper; 'General Electric has an overactive imagination'; 3 October 2018; https://www.ft.com/content/b0060c92-c64a-11e8-ba8f-ee390057b8c9; Accessed on 12 April, 2019

successors are trying to protect themselves from investor criticism without directly blaming their predecessors. The situation is delicate and the chances of getting it wrong are quite high. Much of the challenge is centred on the ambiguous relationship between an outgoing CEO and an incoming CEO. But this raises some important questions.

THE PREDECESSOR'S THOUGHTS ON UPCOMING DEPARTURE

Succession debuted on HBO on 3 June 2018, inspired by the succession tales at Rupert Murdoch's former Twenty First Century Fox and Sumner Redstone's Viacom. Good succession requires the choice of a successor, but equally, a gracefully departing predecessor, who looks forward to quiet anonymity or glory in another sphere. Successful leaders are easily persuaded by sycophants that competent successors are not available or not ready yet.

The harsh truth is that, in almost every case, it is the retiring leader who has made it so! According to research, in almost all cases, the non-availability of a successor is a failure of the predecessor. Two academics, James Champy and Nitin Nohria, wrote, 'To feel threatened by one's successor is a futile but remarkably common reaction to inevitable departure.'

At Hindustan Lever, Prakash Tandon took the top job in 1961. Thereafter, he was followed by Vasant Rajadhyaksha,

T. Thomas, Ashok Ganguly, Susim Datta and several others till today. The distinctive aspect of each transition was that the succession included a clean exit of the predecessor from the affairs of the company.

Louis Begley's novel, *About Schmidt* was made into an Academy Award-winning film in 2002, starring Jack Nicholson. Warren Schmidt retires from his managerial position in a life insurance company, but found it difficult to adjust to life thereafter. He visits his young successor periodically to offer advice and help, but his overtures are politely declined. Seeking meaning in life, he sponsored a Tanzanian child. He disapproves of his daughter's choice of life partner. Despite his professional accomplishments, Schmidt begins to wonder whether he will be remembered for having made a difference to anyone.

Don't we see too many Warren Schmidts in real life?

In the Mahabharata, the story of King Yayati is illustrative of this. He was a fine and successful king, who worked very hard for success. Due to certain events, he was cursed by a holy man to age prematurely. His reprieve from the curse was to persuade one of his sons, a future successor, to swap age with him. The youngest son agreed. King Yayati enjoyed the fruits of youth all over again. After spending all of his years, Yayati reflected on his life and experiences. It had taken Yayati a whole life to realize, 'Not all the food, wealth and women of the world can appease a man of uncontrolled senses.'

In *Leaving on Top: Graceful Exits for Leaders* (2012), ex-Marine, teacher and author David Heenan stated that most leaders could be characterized into four existing types.

- 'Timeless wonders' have great skills, are still relevant and have no reason to call it quits.
- 'Ageing despots' are reluctant to leave.
- 'Comeback kids' return to resurrect their company.
- 'Graceful exiters' quit while still ahead, leaving behind a sterling reputation.

Heenan shared his five-point wisdom and exiting lessons for the predecessor: know your situation, take risks, build networks, continue to be curious, and use instinct to know when to walk away. The tendency to continue, to yearn for what one has left behind is not new.

On 25 May 2018, CNBC carried an article by Bill George, Harvard Senior Fellow.[2] Knowing a bit about Unilever, I read the piece very carefully, '…Unilever has risen above the pack…everything traces to the leadership of Paul Polman for the past decade…turning a moribund company into a powerhouse.' Without doubt, Paul Polman had a vision and an execution plan—kudos to him and his team. He also had the freedom to execute under the superintendence of the board. It takes many years to judge the success of a succession.

---

[2]Bill George; 'As consumer giants struggle, Unilever rises above the pack'; 25 May 2018; https://www.cnbc.com/2018/05/25/bill-george-as-consumer-giants-struggle-unilever-rises-above-the-pack.html
Accessed on 12 April, 2019

Former Unilever Chairman Mike Angus once said, 'The success of my judgement of a CEO candidate is visible only when the *chosen CEO's successor is regarded as successful.*' Testing against that lofty standard, several successions show cracks.

The relationship between predecessor and successor

Frankly, there is no universal rule. First, there may be no relationship at all, and the predecessor may walk away into the sunset as seen in companies like Unilever and GE, where the new CEOs have found their own spaces. Alternatively, the predecessor may stay in with a formal, paid position as non-executive chairman or a paid advisor, as was seen at P&G when A.G. Lafley stayed on as non-executive chairman. So too at L&T and ITC Ltd in India, where it was not the tradition, but was done for the first time in 2016. In ITC, it began as a three year mentoring relation, but was soon extended for another three years, leaving most observers questioning whether continued control was masquerading as mentoring. While there are critics of this practise, it is followed by some.

Some take the view that a more structured process is necessary to tap into the outgoing CEO's intuitive knowledge of the organization. He or she would definitely understand the rational and operational aspects, but would also have an intuitive feel for the organizational and people aspects. To use an architectural metaphor, the outgoing CEO would know the load-bearing pillars in the house. Such companies try to establish a formal relationship for transition. At Intel, for example, the process has been structured and has been strictly followed from Gordon Moore to Andy Grove to Craig Barrett to Paul Otellini. In some companies, the outgoing CEO stays on as a non-executive chairman or a paid advisor in the third category. The successor may build a loose and informal relationship voluntarily for his benefit. For example, in Hindustan Lever, the incoming chairman voluntarily chose to keep an informal link—a drink or a private lunch—and use a former chairman as a sounding board. The final decision would be the incumbent Chairman's, needless to add. I observed that every chairman followed this as an inherited practise.

We have a fourth category in India where many large companies are family-managed. Therefore, the question of ignoring or not consulting the non-executive chairman does not arise, as in Bharti or GoAir. Such family chairmen are non-executive only by designation, because even a fly cannot move within the company without their support and nod. Those that are family-managed make sure that the family is fully involved, and the CEO is selected on the basis that the person accepts this situation. A retiring professional CEO may or may not have a continued role.

Electricity in the connecting wires

Does the incoming CEO need his or her predecessor's advice? My experience is that there is little evidence that the incoming CEO considers consultation with the predecessor a priority. People who rise to be CEOs suffer from flashes of narcissism, if they are not dripping with it. They want to be their own person, and, in many cases, are encouraged by the board to be so. Psychologists say that the incoming CEO is not greatly interested in periodic consultation with the predecessor.

There is also a practical problem of logistics and diary-matching. Nowadays, the predecessor does not simply enjoy his or her retirement by playing golf and sipping vodka by the beach. If the incoming CEO desires to meet, the predecessor may not be easily available and delays due to diaries and logistics further aggravate the congenial motivation to meet. This gives the successor the impression that the predecessor is playing hard-to-get. I know of a case where the incoming CEO found that, despite his best efforts, the predecessor was perpetually abroad. It became impossible to meet with the predecessor and secure focused discussion time, so he stopped trying to meet the predecessor. Massive alienation followed soon after.

And does the exiting leader really want to advise the successor? In a few cases, the answer is an emphatic yes—maybe because the past CEO really believes that he or she can play a role, or maybe because he or she owns a piece of the company. Hank Greenberg ran American International Group (AIG) for forty years. When the 2008 crisis in the financial markets threatened AIG, Greenberg pressed the AIG management for a meeting to advise them, but he was rebuffed, as reported by *The Wall Street Journal*.[3]

However, sometimes the outgoing CEO is also not very keen to offer views to the successor—perhaps because he or she is too proud to hang around the newcomer, waiting to be consulted. He/she is not free of narcissism, and leaders in many other companies seek and pay for his or her advice with great commitment—far more so than the successor CEO. So, unless the outgoing CEO has a formal position to mentor or guide the incumbent, there is not much electricity in the connecting wire.

Writing about CEO departures in his book, *The Hero's Farewell*, Prof Jeffrey Sonnenfeld described the end of an illustrious career as 'a plunge into the abyss of insignificance, a kind of mortality.'

CLEAN-UP JOB

Does a successor have to clean up the predecessor's mistakes? Yes, for sure. It is good to remember that the mess, if any, has probably been contributed to by several predecessors, not one single person—think of bank non-performing assets (NPAs) as an example.

No predecessor can leave a clean slate for the successor. This is part of enterprise and entrepreneurship. This has

---

[3]Liam Pleven; 'Ex-CEO Greenberg's offer got AIG cold-shoulder; *The Wall Street Journal*; https://www.wsj.com/articles/SB122161286853245983 Accessed on 12 April 2019

been admitted by Dara Khosrowshahi, the CEO who took over from Uber founder, Travis Kalanick. 'My predecessor made mistakes. I am going to make mistakes as well. The fact is that I have inherited a fabulous company with fabulous people,' he said in a recent interview. It does not look likely that Khosrowshahi will have a light load for quite a long time to come.

Jeff Immelt struggled with GE for many years, yet the board acted to replace him a few months before the end of his long term. Immelt's successor, John Flannery, got just a year and the board replaced him. Debates are raging about how far back the problems go, and the legendary Jack Welch's record in office is now being reopened. Under Jack Welch and Jeff Immelt, the company executed major initiatives for the future—including entry into businesses like broadcasting, financial services and healthcare. GE made several acquisitions for which it paid top dollar. However, according to critics, GE failed to integrate those acquisitions; the promised delivery of value did not accrue to the GE shareholder. The acquisition of the power company, Alstom, impressed dealmakers, but yielded nothing after being acquired. Building businesses is a long-term game requiring consistency of purpose. GE leaders are thought to have instead become obsessed with their personal legacy and how they wished to be remembered, somewhere down the years.

There are very few companies where an incoming CEO will not have a clean-up job to do. The challenge is to clean up quietly, professionally and without blame.

But can the clean-up job be done quietly? The clean-up has to be done, and doing it discreetly is highly desirable—but not always possible. It is better to clean up visibly early on in the successor's tenure, than be so discreet that the successor gets blamed!

Mistakes are like stocks in a warehouse. There will always be opening stocks, fresh mistakes and closing stock. The incumbent CEO must be convinced about the opportunity he or she has, to do the job at hand; the outgoing CEO's mistakes should not prevent him or her from leading a successful team. The outgoing CEO may be regarded as a hero or a demi-god, as was the case in GE—and that certainly makes the task at hand a delicate one. On the other hand, the mess may come into the public domain. In that case, the CEO can address the issues speedily and in a focused manner. Here are some practical suggestions to consider.

   i. Do not criticize the predecessor, as far as possible. If the successor does the clean-up quietly and without offence, then things will work out fine. If he or she is perceived to blame the predecessor, then it may turn into a crisis. The analyst calls, quarterly results and media routine, however, do place a pressure on the incoming CEO to state what has to be stated within a few months, take the hit and proceed further.
  ii. Square up your perceptions with the principal or promoter director(s). They should get as few

surprises as possible. Seek their guidance, if not their understanding. However, in this process, the CEO must ensure that he or she does not become the scapegoat.

iii. Do not overpromise your management team about achieving dramatic results in an unrealistic time frame. They know the company, its fault lines, and how much time would be required to fix them. Don't try to be a hero to them. If you come across to your employees as a superman, then you have not done well.

iv. Focus on building strong relationships within the company—with new subordinates, business partners and management as a whole. The employees are the people who know what requires fixing in the hidden plumbing and wiring of the organization. Often CEOs are extremely preoccupied with the tensions of dealing with the mess. They know that they have to communicate and manage relations, with the employees, directors, promoters and the external stakeholders. Their preoccupation may cause them to miss out on strengthening their strongest allies, the employees, who will have the firmest ideas on how to solve the problems.

v. Count on your moral authority apart from your hierarchical position. A governance system can function if it is built on a strong moral foundation in a company. The civil engineering principle is relevant—poor foundation, wobbly skyscraper!

Tata has several companies within its group. Not all of them can claim to have implemented a sound succession plan. However, some have indeed followed fine processes, if one were to judge from the smoothness of succession and the outcomes—particularly that there was not only successor planning, but also planning for the smooth exit of the predecessor, as with many MNCs.

For example, Xerxes Desai retired as CEO of Titan. Bhaskar Bhat became his successor. Xerxes had no role in the company after his retirement as CEO and Bhasker led the company with independence and great distinction for well over a decade. Bhasker's successor has now been announced.

Likewise, with TCS: FC Kohli virtually set up the company and, in 1996, was succeeded by S. Ramadorai. Ramadorai ran the company with great distinction for about thirteen years and groomed N. Chandrasekaran, who succeeded him. Chandrasekaran in turn had a ready successor when he was called to helm Tata Sons.

In terms of corporate governance, succession planning counts among the major weaknesses of corporate India. It is, for sure, important to plan a fine bench strength of potential successors. Several companies do so successfully, and HR consultancy companies assist their clients in this exercise. However, that is only one half of the exercise. No predecessor exit planning is attempted by most companies, and few consultancy companies assist with this. The reality is that the predecessor must have a desire to exit in a complete and clean manner. Alarm bells should ring when the board wants the predecessor to continue or when the predecessor demonstrates a desire to hang on for another five years as a mentor. In most situations, it is a bad practise.

6

Making 'Little India' Shine

Institutions like Tata and Hindustan Unilever have transformed the way the Indian economy creates value and builds prosperity for the nation's 1.25 billion citizens. In fact, corporate India has been a catalyst in the remarkable growth of our GDP in the last thirty years since liberalization, which has lifted over 300 million people from abject poverty. This renaissance of our economy has also been driven by the deregulation of the organized sector by 'liberating' the people in 1,200 larger cities (that is, with populations over 50,000).

But sadly this 'breathless' growth has not turned the fortunes of the residents of the over 600,000 small towns and villages in India with populations less than 50,000. This 'Little India', as I call it, has not experienced the highs implied in campaigns such as 'India Shining' or 'Incredible India@60'.

Little wonder then that despite this rapid growth, India's per capita GDP had lagged behind China for all of these past three decades—even though, during the early nineties, both countries had a similar per capita GDP. India's per capita GDP compares with some of the less well-performing countries in the world. As the rest of us take small steps that will culminate in a giant leap forward for India, there are 800 million people in Little India who continue to languish in the clutches of a centralized and bureaucratic system. So while the natural enterprise of large-town India was unshackled by the liberalization of the 1990s, Little India has benefited less, despite the fact that society in the small towns and villages has been self-governing for a large part of history. The centralized form of governance adopted after Independence has shackled the natural enterprise of the people in Little India.

Sadly, this critical aspect of Little India continues to be much the same as before. So, if all our approaches to spreading prosperity over the last seventy years have failed isn't it high time that we try a different, intuitive and natural approach for better results? We need to liberate Little India by empowering people, letting them make their own choices and promoting more local governance. I have always believed that enterprise and decentralization are two sides of the same coin. Whether in a company or a country, enterprise and innovation are promoted by decentralizing authority and empowering people. That is the only way to spread prosperity to larger sections of our population, because it will unleash the natural enterprise of the people out there. This is an approach that Ardeshir Darabshaw Shroff (1899-1965), a director of Tata Sons until 1960, would dearly have loved to see.

A STAUNCH BELIEVER IN ENTERPRISE

Shroff was actively considered for appointment as India's Finance Minister in the 1950s, but never became one. Some decades later, another Tata Director, Nani Palkhivala, was referred to as 'the Finance Minister India never had'. Lest I give the impression that Tata directors routinely miss out on such opportunities, I should clarify that two Tata directors did become Finance Ministers soon after independence—Ghulam Mohammad in Pakistan and John Mathai in India.

During the 1930s, despite the Governor's support, Shroff had been passed over for the post of Deputy Governor of the RBI. Shroff wrote to the governor, 'I am unfortunately too conscious of the fact that the views I have expressed on public matters cannot be acceptable to the Government, but whatsoever others may think of it, frankly speaking, it does not matter two brass buttons to me. I have so far not sought any patronage from government officials, nor do I intend to.'

Shroff was not just uniquely outspoken, but was entrepreneurial and a financial genius. He was a staunch believer in enterprise as a vehicle of economic development.

When he set up the Forum of Free Enterprise in 1956, he wished to educate the public about the infinite capacity of the individual to rise to his or her full potential, given a fertile and conducive environment with minimal controls and regulation. Shroff had said, '...every individual in this country should have the largest possible scope for making his or her contribution towards the development of the country by the use of his or her initiative and enterprise...'

He was also hugely sceptical of a centralized bureaucracy. He did not regard the government schemes for rural development too kindly, as illustrated by his statement from the 1930s, 'Sir James Griggs's clap-trap grants for rural upliftment are once again a tragic repetition of aimless spending which cannot bring us maximum return for every rupee of our slender resources.'

An irreverent commentator could say the same today with considerable accuracy!

'LITTLE INDIA' HAS BEEN BYPASSED

I offer a few indicators to support the almost self-evident view that Little India has gained little from the high national economic growth of recent years:

- One-third of our 650 million rural people live in sparingly electrified villages, despite the technical and tactical claims of various governments. Our government's eagerness to declare victory vastly exceeds the performance on the ground. State and Centre have to work together when it comes to electricity. In recent years, the Centre has governed with antipathy and bad relations with states. An impending Information and Communications Technology (ICT) revolution in the villages is a delusion under these circumstances.

- Surveys on rural poverty and agricultural projects suggest that the government, or its accountability, is practically absent in many villages. In spite of the existence of multiple schemes, periodic surveys of villages in various states suggest that the villagers had never even heard of government schemes such as the implementation of the minimum support price (MSP). Here again, it comes down to state-centre relationships and collaborations.
- Some years ago, the National Commission for Enterprises in the Unorganized Sector (NCEUS) released a report on 'conditions of work and promotion of livelihood in the unorganized sector.' The chairman of the commission stated that 'three fourths of India's population has indeed been bypassed by the high rate of economic growth.'
- Nine tenths of land in India is subject to disputes over ownership. In connection with one such land dispute, two Supreme Court judges, A.K. Mathur and Markandey Katju, had made a strong observation,

about ten years ago: 'People are disgusted with this state of affairs and are losing faith in the judiciary because of the inordinate delay in disposal of cases.' The World Bank has noted that it takes 425 to 1165 days, depending on the state, to enforce a contract in Indian courts.

I have been travelling into Little India for four decades—my eyes and ears tell me what I believe to be true. Although Nehru had said in 1947, 'Everything can wait, but not agriculture,' sixty years later, things are not as the first Prime Minister had dreamt. We need an economic movement that starts in villages, not one that bypasses them.

ENTERPRISING INDIANS

An enterprising community is characterized by an outward-looking attitude and a willingness to explore new ideas as well as to accept exogenous influences. These characteristics have been vibrant in our history through the centuries.

Merchants from Harappa and Mohenjo Daro and were trading with Sumeria as early as 2300 BC. Fa Hien and Hiuen Tsang travelled extensively during the seventh century and recorded their valuable observations. In 1498, as noted by Vasco da Gama, Calicut was already a thriving port city that was familiar to Arab and Chinese merchants.

In 1608, an English captain named William Hawkins dropped anchor at Surat. Armed with 25,000 pieces of gold and a letter from King James I to Emperor Jahangir, he travelled from Surat to Delhi and wrote in his tour report, 'Nothing that England makes at this time is really desired by Indian merchants or officials.'

Over the next 150 years, history has recorded how dramatically events changed. Robert Clive was investigated by the English Parliament for personal enrichment during his years in India. In self-defence, Clive said with feigned humility, 'I walked through vaults which were thrown open to me alone, piled on either hand with gold and jewels! Mr Chairman, at this moment, I stand astonished at my own moderation.'

India was fortunate to never become totally isolated from global influences during its long history. This is quite unlike her Asian neighbours like Japan, Korea and China, all of whom have had at least a couple of centuries of complete isolation from the rest of the world during their history, between 1500 and 1800 AD.

One tends to think of enterprise predominantly in an economic dimension, but it has a social and behavioural dimension as well. In one type of society, an action may be considered enterprising, but not so in another: for example, the opening of a tea shop by a tribal person may be considered enterprising in his immediate social circle, but the same action may not be so for a young man from a trading community.

Enterprise is a creative and innovative response to

the environment. David McClelland established the now widely accepted view that enterprise is promoted by a high achievement orientation, which can be promoted by enriching people's thoughts and fantasies with the language of achievement.

Four factors influence entrepreneurship. First, the experiences that an individual undergoes, and second, the traditions of the family and society in which he lives—both of which impact his attitude to enterprise. Third are the support systems of finance and vocational training/extension services, so he is equipped to become entrepreneurial. Fourth and last is the governmental policy framework, which needs to be supportive and mentoring. These ideas are quite well established and understood.

In the 1960s, there was considerable interest in achieving rapid economic development through small enterprise all over the world. In India, the Small Industry Extension Training Institute (SIETI) was set up and has done positive work over the decades. In reality, the government became the 'mai-baap' or sole parental authority and set up multiple government agencies trying to do the same thing. These agencies have also become bureaucratized and lethargic, whereas what is needed is a purposeful effort to promote small town/village enterprise. The flip side of an enterprising people is that they are empowered and decentralized. That too has been an Indian tradition.

R. GOPALAKRISHNAN

THE GOVERNMENT-LESS CIVILIZATION

The erudite statesman, C. Rajagopalachari, wrote that India had probably the largest number, and very big time-lengths, of intervals between one effective government and another; and that there have been a great many periods during which the people had neither central nor regional governments exercising effective authority. All these periods of what may be called a no-government condition could not possibly have been tided over but for the self-restraints imposed by our culture.

This gene of enterprise prospered for centuries under a government-less system in which small communities managed their interests locally. In terms of governance, India has, for the longest time, been a multiplicity of village communities. Excluding five of the twenty-five centuries of recorded history, a centralized bureaucratic state in India was a rarity.

Power was not embodied in the concept of the state. Rulers ruled by capturing the symbolic seat of power. They preferred extracting taxes over fundamentally changing the societies in their kingdoms. As Charles Metcalfe wrote, 'The village communities seem to last when nothing else lasts. Dynasty after dynasty tumbles down; revolution succeeds revolution; Hindu, Pathan, Mughal, Maratha, Sikh, English are masters in turn, but the village communities remain the same.'

I struggle for a modern metaphor to imagine how things might have been. The situation might be analogous to a corporate conglomerate or the portfolio of a financial investor. In either case, the prime motivation is economic reward rather than changing the institutions fundamentally. Individual companies are bought and sold, but the managers carry on running their companies as best as they can. Similarly, Indian society carried on, somewhat unmindful of who was ruling and collecting taxes.

Around the time of Aurangzeb, India was not an integrated market for goods and services due to three barriers—an underdeveloped road and river system, the danger of being looted while moving goods across the geography, and the levying of customs taxes at multiple points during the transit of goods. That is why India was a conglomerate of regional markets.

At the time of Independence, apart from colonial India, there were more than 500 princely states—the larger ones even having their own currency, stamps and railways. The integration of these states, thanks to Vallabhbhai Patel and V.P. Menon, has been such a staggering achievement that modern Indians have almost forgotten that just sixty years ago, we were not one country but 500; further, that 300 years ago, we were an agglomeration of multiple village communities.

Without doubt, of course, there was a larger and more cohesive power across the peninsula as embodied by culture and religion. I do not underestimate the unifying importance of culture and religion when I refer to decentralized governance.

When the Indian constitution was developed during the 1940s, there was considerable debate on centralization versus decentralization. The constitution ended up leaning towards centralization, which was an adaptation of western principles to suit our situation and for which, an enabling colonial system was in place. The unfortunate violence of partition also must have tipped opinions in favour of centralization.

In fiscal matters, in particular, the effects of such a centralizing move were feared to be deleterious. Leaders like K. Santhanam of Madras argued that these fiscal provisions would make the states 'beggars at the door of the Centre.' Well, he has turned out to be right.

The Constitution was amended in 1993, making it mandatory to elect village panchayat leaders every five years, one-third of whom have to be women. This means that over three million legislators are elected in India every five years, a humongous democratic feat unparalleled in the world.

However, the village panchayats have little flexibility in raising funds. That is why we have MLAs thronging state capitals, and MPs thronging Delhi—to lobby, bully and argue for financial allocations instead of working in their constituencies for their electorates.

The issue of centralization versus decentralization is alive even today.

LITTLE INDIA'S CHANGE AGENDA

India has had so much regulation that no amount of deregulation seems adequate. The chambers of commerce still conduct conferences on subjects like 'Is India Inc. over-regulated?' If India Inc. thinks so, imagine the situation in Little India.

There are several instances that reinforce the feeling of hopelessness among the small town/rural population—about the lack of rural infrastructure, banks, schools, healthcare or transport to nearby towns, all of which are essential to support commerce and enterprise and the creation of jobs. I have travelled into small towns and villages to assess these feelings. I have been shocked to find a story of economic deprivation, social injustice and hopelessness that big town folks like me cannot comprehend.

Citizens who have worked in Little India have experienced these shocking standards of public service and governance. 'For more than fifty years, successive governments have initiated several programs to deal with poverty, but they have not made a sufficiently major dent in the economic and social status of hundreds of millions,' observes one such worker.

The various public schemes are not entirely useless; but the state of public services undertaken by corrupt governments and inefficient bureaucracies is far below the community's needs. The solution lies in leveraging the natural spirit of enterprise among the people of Little India by empowering them further. Intuitively, this sounds like a worthy approach.

Intellectuals and bureaucrats in urban areas make the decisions about Little India. They are intrinsically more interested in subjects like organized industry, foreign investment, stock markets and so on. The issue of Little India's economic growth continues to be only partially attended. Something has to change. But having tried other alternatives in the past, it is now time to do something different.

However, we need a different trajectory in setting the agenda for change. Unlike industrial licensing, which unshackled industry in a swift manner, Little India's change agenda will be somewhat evolutionary, being rooted in society and politics. But the time has come.

Robert Reich, a professor of public policy, observes, 'Democracy means more than a process of free and fair elections. Democracy is a system for accomplishing what can only be achieved by citizens joining together with other citizens.' The role of capitalism is to enlarge the economic pie. The slicing up of the economic pie is the role of governance and democracy.

IMPORTANT LESSONS

The Department of Economics and Statistics in Tata Services (DES) undertook a study on entrepreneurship in Little India about five years ago. I shall mention a few salient features of the study.

The aim was to understand the nature of entrepreneurship, and the barriers and triggers to enterprise in small places. Approximately 1,200 small entrepreneurs were interviewed in and around twelve village clusters in the four regions of India.

The study suggests a model for sparking enterprise in small towns and villages. It has four drivers: Infrastructure (roads, electricity, and water), Finance and Facilitation (loans, helpful officials), 'Rural MBA' (training on markets and basic commerce) and Social Capital (health, education, hope).

Reassuringly, this model is similar to the David McClelland findings referred to earlier. Two activities were found to dominate enterprise—about 50 per cent are engaged in commercial farming (farming for the market rather than consumption) and 20 per cent in Rural Non-Farm Services (RNFS). Incidentally, the RNFS sector is a fast growing rural job generator and holds much promise for the future.

The findings are interesting in five aspects:

1. Panchayat leaders and local politicians, whom urban folks tend to trash, are seen as quite helpful in promoting enterprise.
2. Bank officials are also perceived as helpful. Admittedly, this is a partial view because the banking system has rather limited reach. As per National Sample Survey Office (NSSO) data, half of farming households do not access any credit, whether from institutional

or non-institutional sources. Even among farmer borrowers, there is more recourse to non-institutional sources than the banking sector.
3. The people out there are crying out for vocational training in business—a sort of 'rural MBA', if a loose term can be used.
4. The perception is that the environment for enterprise has hardly changed. A plausible explanation for this paradox is that perhaps those funds and schemes do not quite reach those they are intended for.
5. There seems to be a robust self-confidence and common-sense about what it takes to be successful in enterprise.

Perhaps the folks in Little India will surprise the nation through their enterprise just as they have done in matters of voting and politics.

Some years ago, Rallis India conducted a survey among 1,200 villagers across twenty villages each in six different states. To a question about the kind of activities already being undertaken by the panchayat, the top three responses were: overhauling village infrastructure, resolution of disputes, and help with water issues. This too suggests the desire and willingness on the part of Little India to do more things locally.

Here, I would like to share some valuable lessons documented by the Head of Community Services in the Tata Chemicals Rural Development Society (TCRDS).

TCRDS cooperated with the International Centre for Entrepreneurship and Career Development (ICECD), an institution established in 1986. It is located at Ahmedabad and is recognized as a centre of excellence by the United Nations; it has trained over 10,000 people, who in turn have developed the enterprise capabilities of thousands. The focus is to promote enterprise, particularly among women. Using the training imparted by ICECD to their staff, TCRDS conducted a sort of 'rural MBA' program for the forty-two villages around Mithapur in local community halls, private rooms or wherever convenient.

TCRDS has drawn certain lessons from its experiences. One such lesson is that the government can become a threat to entrepreneurs when they become successful—as in the case of a woman entrepreneur, who attracted the attention of the sales tax department. Another lesson is the role of society. In Gujarat, enterprise is perceived positively, but not so in Babrala, Uttar Pradesh, where caste determines what can be done and by whom. A third lesson is the need for a facilitating information cell, something akin to a Tata Vyavasai Kendra.

One of the Tata companies, Tata BP Solar in Bangalore, makes and markets solar panels. I was quite struck by their work. I was interested to learn that apart from its green credentials, solar power in villages has three benefits—improved access to electricity, providing direct employment to install and maintain the panels, and collecting electricity charges at a periodic frequency; it also generates indirect employment through small fabrication shops, outlets to sell solar-powered household devices, storage, transport, etc. Tata BP Solar estimates that the direct plus indirect employment potential could be about 700 people per megawatt of solar power. Of the over 200,000 MW needed in the country, even if only 5,000 MW were to come from solar power, the direct and indirect employment potential in Little India could be 3.5 million! This employment level is impressive when compared to the 13 million jobs (direct plus indirect) generated by the auto industry or the 2 million direct jobs generated by the IT and IT-enabled services (ITeS) industry. The people in the 600,000+ towns and villages of Little India need both the electricity and the jobs.

THE CHALLENGE OF SCALABLE EXPERIENCES

There are several examples of enterprise in small places. The most prominent is the Khadi Village Industries Corporation (KVIC). About 8 million workers serve full or part time, earning a total of ₹5,000 crores as wages between them and selling ₹14,000 crores of merchandise. Without detailing the valuable initiatives themselves, mentioning just a few examples might illustrate my point about the difficulty of scalability:

Chetna Gala Sinha runs a 'Mann Deshi Udyogini', that provides vocational and financial training to help women become entrepreneurs and access the benefits of micro-entrepreneurship.

Due to power shortages disrupting trade in Sheetlamata Sabji Mandi at Khamla near Nagpur, garage owner Panju Totwani installed a 7.5 kw generator set for the vegetable traders.

The challenge, however, is to scale up and transfer such examples. Without transference and scale, such initiatives stay local.

Governments respond by allocating more funds and setting up more schemes, which continue to run through a centralized bureaucracy. As a result, there are overlapping schemes run by many ministries at the state and federal levels: I once counted over fifty schemes from the central government alone, amounting to over ₹50,000 crores. As mentioned earlier, even the awareness of such schemes tends to be low among the villagers.

THE CHALLENGE OF DECENTRALIZATION

Everyone wants decentralization, but only up to their level. The reality is that markets for land, credit and agro-produce have to be encouraged to develop. Otherwise, as Hernando de Soto has written engagingly, people will never be empowered. That is why India must decentralize further and faster. How? In preparation for the Eleventh Plan, the Ministry of Panchayati Raj set up an expert group on planning at the grassroots level. The group has addressed many aspects of policy reform. Their report deals with reforms in the planning process right from the village level and its coordination at the district level by the District Planning Committees.

'While fifty-five years of planning has failed to deliver social and economic services at the desired levels and efficiency, perhaps decentralizing the planning is the only option left and, hopefully, this report will not merely find the place in the shelves,' wrote the Director of the National Institute of Public Finance and Policy (NIFPP).

An impediment to decentralization is the authority to raise local revenue. If this is not granted to them, then locally-elected people will forever be hanging around higher-level offices to negotiate and get allocated funds for their local needs. That is why village level leaders flock to district offices, district officials flock to state capitals and state officials flock to Delhi! In this context, the Bombay Chamber have mooted a good idea. They have identified a completely new source of revenue, the raising of which, they propose, can be mandated to the panchayats, who are also well qualified to do so. In this way, there will not be any interference with any ongoing revenue raising or usage scheme. The idea can use the instinctive capability of self-governance by local bodies to raise and manage funds for village enterprise or the public good.

The paper pointed out that the total land revenue of *all* states at the time of the report in 2010 was ₹2,295 crores. Bengal alone accounted for 32 per cent of this. If other states could raise revenue in line with Bengal, then the panchayat bodies could raise ₹25,000 crores. This money can be used for developing village level infrastructure and promoting enterprise in small places. It is certainly a novel idea worthy of further development, as commented upon by a newspaper.

Another impediment in decentralization is the tendency of muscle power and caste to play a role in elections. A thought provoking paper has been written to explain why people elect the same leaders despite their known proclivity to extract rent from the system. Especially where communities are divided by caste and religion, the fear that a new leader may come from a different community restrains people from voting out their 'own man'. That is why, in India, we find that criminals are included among our council of ministers and 'important people' are never jailed.

The truth is that we may well be brewing a crisis. There are six symptoms of a brewing crisis:

- Leaders know that a problem exists and that the problem will not solve itself.
- Leaders recognize that the problem is getting worse over a period of time.
- Fixing the problem will cost a lot today but the benefits will come much later.
- One leader will incur this cost but another will reap the benefits.
- There is a tendency to fix a few short term things than address the *real* issues.

- Inaction benefits a minority which thwarts the leadership's efforts.

All these six symptoms are evident and clearly visible to many of us. The solution lies in releasing the enterprise of the people in Little India and empowering them. Whatever is to be done must be different and done with a sense of urgency.

A.D. Shroff was so frenetic a worker that his doctor once told him, 'You are like a woman who wants to have a baby but cannot wait nine months!' That is the spirit of urgency we need.

7

The Future of Agriculture Is Not in the Stars

It isn't just Little India that has suffered years of neglect. In the current frenzy of Start-up India, Digital India and Skill India, it appears that we may have inadvertently left Bharat and rural India behind, thus deepening an existing cleavage. Evidence stares at us through the reports of rural distress, farmers' suicides and morchas. New technologies and outlooks like targeted irrigation, better seeds, soil management and digitizing offer an unprecedented opportunity to transform agricultural and rural India, which is the source of half the jobs in the country and exports worth $40 billion.

A quick historical recap about the national approach to agriculture may be in order. After Nehru's death, the Congress party elected Lal Bahadur Shastri to be the next Prime Minister. Shastri offered the agriculture portfolio to

Neelam Sanjeeva Reddy, who turned it down for various reasons. Firstly, earlier incumbents like Jairamdas Daulatram, K.M. Munshi and Rafi Ahmed Kidwai had won little acclaim; secondly, agriculture had a poor image compared to industry; and thirdly, since Independence, this portfolio had had no takers. Shastri called on Chidambaram Subramaniam (CS) and requested him to take up the agriculture portfolio. Having served as the minister for Steel and Heavy Industry, CS wondered whether he had been demoted.[1]

Clearly, this episode reinforces the view that although agriculture is India's most important economic and political subject, it is not well regarded for influence and, therefore, not much sought after. It is about time that India makes the Agriculture Minister a sort of czar among ministers. There have been about sixty-five budget speeches since Independence; without exception, each one has emphasised the importance of agriculture and announced a few measures in bits and pieces, like subsidies, loan waivers, water body renewals and minimum support prices (MSP). Maybe things will change in the future, as the current state of farming cannot simply carry on. Notwithstanding these big-ticket announcements, I believe it is time for mindful and intelligent agriculture—'Sarthak Krishi'.

---

[1] *Hand of Destiny*, volume 2, Bharatiya Vidya Bhavan

A HELICOPTER VIEW

To achieve this, I would like to recommend three fundamental ideas: first, I wish to promote the idea of 'conceptual frameworks' as generally being important in transformation management (think of the framework for industrial development in the years after Independence as an example); second, I suggest a framework specifically for the transformation of farming; and third, I assert that advances in information and biological technologies, like digitizing land records, soil conditions and genetic modification, offer a rare opportunity to make a huge leap. It is a helicopter view of an incredibly complex subject; however, the value of a helicopter view should not be underestimated. There are many government committees that have said *what* should be done; for *how* it needs to be done, it may be of benefit to have a National Agricultural Policy Framework.

The framework for farming must be conceptualized to be holistic: dairy, poultry, fisheries, rural development and water management. What follows is a potted history of the evolution of agricultural policy. From Independence till 1965, agriculture was reformed in bits and pieces in an environment of multiple pulls and pressures for resources, from many quarters. For several years, the terms of trade were acknowledged to be adverse for agriculture, compared to industry, before a correction was attempted in the 1990s. At the time of the Annual Session of the Congress at Durgapur in January 1965, a new agricultural policy had not yet been formulated. The absence of a framework does not precipitate crisis, but a general decline may set in. The food crisis of the mid-sixties led to the second phase of this evolution. It was a determined and dogged phase, spearheaded by C. Subramanian, in which enormous success was achieved in leadership of political consensus and in adopting new technologies like dwarf variety of seeds, fertilizer application and pest control. The green revolution phase ran its course until 2000, when a new National Agricultural Policy (NAP) was announced by the Vajpayee government.

The NAP was targeted 'to achieve an agricultural growth of 4 per cent per annum (which has not been achieved till date), to strengthen the rural infrastructure, to offer a decent standard of living to farmers and to speed up value-added agricultural growth.' Thereafter, the UPA set up the National Commission on Farmers in 2004, and its report was submitted in 2006. That is the last we ever heard about an agricultural policy. We do have a lot of bits and pieces, but who is to put the jigsaw together?

I cannot emphasize the importance of putting it together. In managerial terms, frameworks are very important to help participants of any transformation visualize their role in the larger game plan. The issue is—would the participants of the transformation be the proverbial brick layers, or would they be building the cathedral? Management academics, consultants and journals have, over many years, periodically reported about the importance of harmonizing strategy and culture—of putting into place systems, processes and structures—so that leadership can deliver results.

What CS wrote about the situation in 1965 can be repeated with significant validity even now, half a century later: 'I was able to look at agriculture from a completely different perspective. For example, in an industry, no industrial unit can progress or succeed unless it is a profitable concern. After some study, discussion and analysis, [I] came to the conclusion that Indian agriculture was a losing concern for the Indian farmer.'

The reality is that the country does not have an integrated framework to transform agriculture. There is a huge downside to the fragmentation of efforts and leakage of funds arising from too many central ministries and lack of coordination with the states.

FRAMING THE FARMING ISSUE

Unlike industry and telecom, agriculture is a state subject. The solutions, as well as actions, with regard to agriculture tend to get political and fragmented; they do not lend themselves naturally to a holistic design by a single agency. In this context, it is worth noting what Dr Y.K. Alagh has said, 'The future of agriculture is not in the stars, even in a country deeply committed to the inevitability of predictable karmic outcomes...pull together the main analyses and place them in a holistic framework...Indian agriculture responds well to well thought out policy stimuli.'

A holistic national framework to address agricultural problems could derive structural lessons from the way India industrialized. There were four pillars on which the industrialization strategy was based—licensing, skill development, industrial finance and management development. These played out over sixty years—admittedly with flaws and strengths—but today India is counted among the top industrial powers in the world.

Putting together a similar set of the pillars for agriculture is essential to aggregate the wisdom that already exists and to address the development issues that the nation faces. The holistic plan should encompass Technology, Risk, Institutions, Policy and Skills. The nation needs a forward-looking 'Sarthak Krishi Yojana' which encompasses five pillars:

I. Technology incubation: Outcome based technology policy encouraging research, innovation and incubation. This includes setting the policy with regard to digital drivers for agriculture, improved seeds, and soil management, and directing research efforts of the state universities to outcome-based research.

II. Risk institutions and financing: Banks and financial institutions to help promote technology infusion, insurance and mechanisation. This includes the role of the National Bank for Agricultural and Rural

Development (NABARD), insurance companies and rural financial institutions with regard to farmer financing, risk mitigation and insurance.

III. Institutions of governance: Promote Farmer Producers organisations (FPOs) to be agri-focused small and medium or micro, small and medium enterprises (SMEs/MSMEs). This is a dire and central need. India needs 10 million FPOs, like industrial SMEs, rather than 120 million individual farmers. The nation did not industrialize with mom-and-pop craft units—the nation planned SMEs to support large-scale industrialization.

IV. Policy for farming: Focus on improving human and farm productivity. Whatever labour is deployed on the farm must be productive, thus releasing labour for industrial and service sector needs. Farm productivity measures like mechanization and spraying techniques are needed desperately.

V. Skilling: Agricultural Technical Training Institutes (ATIs). This is the equivalent of the ITIs that accompanied industrialization. Farming is conducted in India like a craft, rather than a skill. ATIs, modelled on private-public partnerships, can play the role that ITIs did for India's early industrialization.

Government must articulate the features and components that would constitute these five pillars, seek consensus with states and implement a comprehensive National Agricultural

Mission. This has the chance to instil enthusiasm in the agricultural sector and invite wide participation.

MY PICK OF THE TOP TEN

Granular and detailed suggestions are plentiful in the files of the government. Here is my pick of the top ten measures—well-known, oft repeated and urgent—to be considered within the framework:

   i. Invest political resources to develop a consensus with the states, allowing some chance to execute a national agenda for agriculture. It makes good economic and political sense to do so, irrespective of the political party in power. If half the effort to build consensus for the Goods and Services Tax (GST) had gone into agriculture, the GDP benefits would have a higher impact! To ensure the success of 'Sarthak Krishi Yojana', it should be a collaboratively driven project with the states. For example, the Agriculture Produce Market Committee (APMC) Act has been a stumbling block to freer marketing of produce, and a consensus with the states is essential.
   ii. Increase irrigated area from 48 per cent to 60 per cent over a few years by restoring public investment in rural infrastructure—check-dams and bunds for water, rural roads, warehousing etc.
   iii. Revamp the Minimum Support Price (MSP)

regime, which began as a support but has become a crutch; it has been implemented patchily in the country and it farmers in many states are not even sufficiently aware of it.

iv. Nominate one agency (like NABARD) to encourage the aggregation of land interest and farmer holdings among willing farmers by forming FPOs under the Companies Act. Agriculture needs the equivalent of the SMEs/MSMEs of industry. This single measure will improve financial inclusion, as farmers will become owners of bankable assets.

v. While exercising caution with regard to new technologies like Genetically Modified Organisms (GMO), the present system of political filibustering over science cannot continue. India must rely on a scientific temper and courage of leadership in introducing the required technological vibrancy in Indian agriculture. CS has described how there was enormous resistance to High Yield Variety (HYV) seeds in the 1960s and how he overcame it. Farmer meetings were held by the states, in which farmers were given demonstrations of the effect of the new seeds, following which a planned communication and promotion program was implemented in every state.

vi. Reorient the agricultural science effort to be far more market and farmer-led. CS explains at great length how he attempted this half a century ago. I believe our Indian Council of Agricultural Research (ICAR) laboratories have lost their focus over the decades, and they need a renewal agenda, much like those attempted periodically at Council of Scientific & Industrial Research (CSIR) laboratories.

vii. Rationalize the heavy subsidy regime on fertilizers. The current policy has strangulated the nutrient industry and distorted the national soil map.

viii. Drive the proposed Bima Yojana to rapidly extend insurance cover to more of the 120 million farmers than it does at present.

ix. Include agriculture in the skills efforts of the country by launching Agriculture Technology Training Institutes (ATTIs) just as ITIs were started for industrialization. The same is true of the Make in India program. Is there any reason why India needs only defence and aerospace production and not more efficient food production for export?

x. Just as China has a *Taobao*[2], India must aim to digitally connect the 20 million progressive farmers into a digitally-led transformative road. Private sector start-ups can play a vital role in this national effort. Indeed, several companies, including Rallis India, Syngenta India and several start-ups, are already working in this area.

---

[2] www.taobao.com

No country has achieved a bright overall future without a bright food and agricultural future. India has much work to do, even after decades of Independence. But she can still usher in a new wave of transformation through a planned framework.

8

Navigating the Labyrinth: A Citizen's View of Justice

We have seen how poor incomes, stress and an uncertain future have left a large percentage of India's agrarian society deeply disillusioned with the government. But as citizens, don't we all have expectations from the systems in the country, particularly the justice system?

In fact, there is a sense of irony and disenchantment in my own perspective about our justice system. When I read about the contribution of our judiciary, especially that of our courts in terms of shaping the constitutional law—the foundation that sustains our democracy—and in matters of expanding and advancing citizens' fundamental rights, I find that our judiciary's accomplishments have been sterling. From interpreting the Constitution to evolving the concept of 'institutional integrity' in matters of appointment to high offices, the role of our judiciary has been extraordinary. There are other examples: long before the legislature made a law on prevention of sexual harassment, our Supreme Court, in the Vishakha case, had laid down guidelines for protection of working women from sexual harassment at the workplace. If today the enforcement of environment protection laws gets the attention it deserves, it is largely because of a resolute judiciary which, through a creative use of the tool of Public Interest Litigation (PIL), has been steadfast in protecting the environment. And most importantly, barring a few aberrations in the past, our judiciary has remained fiercely independent and has displayed its independence in no uncertain terms. We can find faults with our justice system, but we, by no means, have a judiciary of 'committed judges', as our politicians periodically seem to desire.

As we saw with the Vodafone tax dispute, it requires a great deal of courage and conviction in the rule of law for a judiciary in any part of the world, especially in a developing country like ours, to set aside a tax demand of over $2 billion. One may disagree with the decision, but the judgement of our Supreme Court in the National Judicial Appointments Commission (NJAC) case was a telling display of the might of an independent judiciary that does not shy away from striking down a constitutional amendment. This amendment was piloted by a government which had been voted to power on the back of a huge electoral mandate. Further, it was an issue which saw an unprecedented political consensus—both Parliament and state legislatures had ratified the amendment almost unanimously.

It would be wrong to assume that if judicial decisions are accepted and implemented, it is only because of the fear of contempt. It is perhaps also because the credibility our judiciary commands in public opinion, and popular perception, is much higher than other institutions of governance. But then, if the credibility of the judiciary as an institution is to be preserved, it is imperative that we not just glorify the accomplishments but also acknowledge and confront the not-so-pleasant realities of our justice delivery system. It is in this spirit that I now present my frank views as a common citizen. I do so with the belief that it is better to be critical of our institutions of justice than be cynical of the system, which we as citizens are increasingly becoming.

THE LONG AND PAINFUL ROAD TO JUSTICE

The pain of delays

The right to seek justice in terms of resolution of disputes is not expressly provided in the Constitution. The Preamble speaks of justice in an egalitarian sense—social, economic and political. But the Supreme Court has interpreted the right to speedy justice as part of the fundamental rights under the Constitution. Therefore, I interpret that the

Indian Constitution assures the citizen the right to receiving reasonable justice in reasonable time. In this context, the meandering ways of the current justice system are totally incomprehensible to the citizen.

The Salman Khan hit-and-run case dates back to 2002, but even as late as 2015, our system was grappling with who was driving the car at the time of the accident. Jessica Lal was murdered in cold blood in 1999. Believe it or not, the murderers were acquitted after seven years. It took sustained action by civil society to have the facts re-examined and secure life imprisonment for the accused. The Aarushi Talwar murder case was incredibly convoluted, but at least it resulted in conviction within five years, though an appeal is pending. Many other criminal cases seem to drag on.

It is only fair for the citizen to wonder about our justice system. It is difficult for them to understand why society has to wait for a couple of decades before a case gets resolved; and if anyone is doing anything to ensure speedy resolution! Citizens may have become cynical about whether certain cases will be resolved at all.

The pain of injustice

The lay citizen certainly feels greatly offended that high level connections and access to top lawyers confers special advantage to some citizens. To the citizens, it appears that Vijay Mallya or Lalit Modi can bask in London, caring two hoots for trial in India, regardless of the facts and the reality. For the public, it is annoying to see Mohammad Shahabuddin, four-time Rashtriya Janata Dal (RJD) Member of Parliament (MP), emerge on parole from jail with a mocking smile after serving sentences for various crimes. It is galling to see former Haryana director general of police (DGP), S.P.S. Rathore, smirk live on television following his sentencing in 2009 for the molestation of fourteen-year-old Ruchika Girhotra in 1990. The young woman committed suicide in 1993. It took nineteen years, forty adjournments and more than four hundred hearings before the court finally pronounced the officer guilty. He was sentenced to six months in prison and a fine of a princely sum of ₹1000. The sentence of six months awarded by the trial magistrate was enhanced by the Sessions Court to one-and-half years, which was affirmed by the High Court. But an appeal was admitted by the Supreme Court in 2010, which took six years to decide, and ultimately reduced the sentence on the grounds of old age. So the accused ultimately got the benefit of a protracted trial and the appeal process, for an offence committed by him more than two decades ago!

The pain of corrupt institutions

There are several public institutions which, together, are meant to ensure an orderly society for citizens. Though their remits, jurisdictions and roles are different, the police, the Central Bureau of Investigation (CBI), regulators and the courts system are all parts of what constitutes, in the citzen's mind, the keepers of order in society. Of course, such public institutions can get corrupted—any institution is prone to corruption. But when the police, the CBI and the judiciary are openly accused of corruption, the citizen gets truly concerned.

The subject of police reform is not new. In a monograph published by Calcutta University in 1913,[1] the very first sentence read, 'Of all the branches of public service in India, the police, by its history and traditions, is the most backward in character.' The eagerness of ministers to exercise control over the Police Department, especially the unbridled desire of the Delhi Chief Minister to get control of the police, and the legions of stories about how politicians meddle with and deter professionalism in police management, have been documented for years.

The apparent incompetence or waywardness of the CBI and its alleged propensity to political manipulation are evidenced by the twists and turns in cases like Bofors and the Kargil coffin scam (or 'coffingate'). But here is the irony: everyone knows about the inefficient judicial process and the perceived corruption of the CBI—yet, in any big case, you hear demands for a judicial probe and investigation by the very same CBI! When politicians demand a CBI probe, aren't they admitting that the normal police force is

---

[1]*History of Police Organization in India and Indian Village Police, Being Select Chapters of the Report of the Indian Police Commission, 1902-1903.* University of Calcutta, 1913.

hopelessly inefficient and ineffective in investigating cases? I believe a CBI probe becomes an excuse to divert attention from the real issue at hand.

Retired Supreme Court judge Markandey Katju aired his views on the judiciary at a public forum in 2015. 'My assessment is that 50 per cent of the higher judiciary has become corrupt.'[2] That his statement has gone unchallenged and undebated so far suggests to the disheartened citizen that, indeed, the judiciary has also become deeply corrupt.

The pain of watching helpless problem-solvers

The citizen thinks that both the responsibility and the authority to solve issues lie with the government and the judiciary. It is appalling to watch a serving Chief Justice of India (CJI) shed tears publicly, and to hear him narrate the constraints under which the judiciary is working. If a company CEO lobbies with banks and the government for temporary concessions to protect his organization from unprecedented difficulties without first improving efficiencies within his company, the CEO would surely cut a poor figure. The CJI's action would have been perfectly acceptable and persuasive if, over the years, CJIs had done everything within their authority to improve the functioning of the courts: for

---

[2] '50% of higher judiciary corrupt, says ex-SC judge Markandey Katju'; *Hindustan Times*, 28 Sep, 2015; https://www.hindustantimes.com/punjab/50-of-higher-judiciary-corrupt-says-ex-sc-judge-markandey-katju/story-Hfu8Ru8o9YfoGOjloboytN.html
Accessed on 18 April, 2019

example, reviewing the number of adjournments allowed, or the length of time provided for arguments to proceed, or the priorities set for hearings in courts.

Indeed, the citizen is aghast upon learning that in 1999, an amendment provided that a maximum of three adjournments could be granted during a suit, or that a court should not extend to more than thirty days the time they grant to perform certain necessary acts. Within six years of that amendment being passed, the Supreme Court ruled in the Salem Advocates Bar Association case that notwithstanding the 1999 amendment, the courts could use their discretion in such matters. No wonder that we have over thirty million cases pending in our courts. I am told that by one calculation, disposal of these cases means that if all of our nation's judges were to work non-stop with no breaks, and dispose of a hundred cases every hour, it would still take thirty-five years to catch up!

So who is to blame? The citizen learns that there is a body called the Law Commission that has been in existence since 1834! This Commission is an executive body whose major function is 'to work for legal reform.' From 1834 until 1947, within 113 years, the colonial government appointed three Law Commissions. Since Independence, the government has appointed twenty-one Law Commissions.

Almost thirty years ago, the 120th report of the Law Commission stated, 'Politically the Indian State, since the colonial period, has self-consciously understaffed the judiciary…adequate reorganization of the Indian Judiciary is at one and the same time [is] everybody's concern and, therefore, nobody's concern… Hungary has seventy Supreme Court judges while India has twenty-five… The Commission recommends that by the year 2000, India should command at least the ratio that the USA commands of 107 judges per million of population…' India is nowhere near the required or recommended numbers in the judiciary. Between 1950 and today, the number of Supreme Court judges went up by four times whereas the number of cases filed in the Supreme Court went up by seventy times!

Apart from the judicial system, the governments over the years do not seem to have considered speedy and efficient judicial proceedings to be important for flagship programs like simplifying business, encouraging entrepreneurship, skilling, or promoting Make in India. How could we have developed such a sclerosis of a mounting backlog of cases, built up over several decades, right under the noses of successive Prime Ministers, Chief Justices, Law Ministers and Law Commissions? Is the citizen not right to be shocked that all these luminaries have not yet addressed the issues regarding the matter?

PERCEPTIONS OF JUSTICE AND INJUSTICE

Feelings of injustice

In Charles Dickens' *Great Expectations,* the key character, Pip, has a rough upbringing under his sister. He faces several injustices as a child. With great pathos, Pip says, 'My sister's bringing up had made me sensitive. In the little world in which children have their existence, whosoever brings them up, there is nothing so finely perceived and finely felt, as injustice. It may be only a small injustice that the child can be exposed to; but the child is small, and its world is small, and its rocking-horse stands so many hands high, according to scale, as a big-boned Irish hunter.'

Like the child, the naïve and common citizen has a simplistic and unidimensional image of justice. The citizen assumes that learned judges listen to learned counsels on the merits of a case, and in a reasonable time, they conclude their views on the matter, though differences do occasionally get expressed. But it is bewildering to the citizen when a retired Supreme Court judge opines on a current judgement, whether the matter pertains to cricket or to a criminal case.

Justice Katju thinks the present judges have erred in their judgement in the 2011 rape and murder case of Soumya, a woman from Kerala. Indeed, he has the right and the competence to have a different view. But his action is perceived by the citizen to be back-seat driving, because there would be mayhem in society if retired judges start expressing dissenting opinions—a privilege reserved for sitting judges, and that too, only judges hearing the matter under consideration. Senior Advocate Fali Nariman has told the court that Justice Katju expressing views from outside will confuse the public. Surely there must be a better way to express alternative views!

Different grounds of injustice

Professor Amartya Sen has argued in his tome, *The Idea of Justice,* that a theory of justice must include ways of determining how to reduce injustice as much as ways of advancing justice. The complication is that people can share a strong sense of injustice, but across many different grounds. The lay public may not have any dominant consensus on the reason for the perceived injustice. This was in full display on the question of how to treat the juvenile accused in the Nirbhaya case.

The rulebook puritans argued that regardless of whether the accused was a juvenile by a week or a year, the facts must prevail. Social reformers argued that large-scale social education was required to rid society of any deviant citizen, whether juvenile or adult. The eye-for-an-eye commentators were vociferous about not hiding behind technicalities and meting out the strongest punishment as though the accused was an adult. I will not recount the many subtle variations of these themes. All of them totally agreed on the injustice of the crime, but they could not agree on the reasoning behind the injustice!

Delusions about 'strong' laws

In the popular imagination, having strong laws is a failsafe deterrent. Indeed, there is some validity to this point of view—but only some! Strong laws must be accompanied by strong enforcement capabilities and capacity building.

Otherwise there is merely an accumulation of strong laws which further complicate an already complex situation. If I might offer the most crass and visible example, consider how well we are able to enforce the rules concerning two wheeler drivers wearing crash helmets or automobile drivers stopping at red lights.

Regulatory agencies clamour the most to be armed with greater powers. The vanishing companies scam of the 1990s and the Ketan Parekh scam a decade later resulted in more powers being given to the Securities and Exchange Board of India (SEBI). The expectations of citizens from regulators also increase as they are given more powers. But for the citizen, the reality turns out to be different. For example, SEBI legislated that company boards should have at least one woman director and that half of the company board membership should be independent directors, yet public sector companies failed to conform to this law. Indeed, SEBI went to the extent of exempting eleven PSUs from following its own law! SEBI itself failed to get a woman director for a long time after it framed the rules for others.

NDTV reported a case which has been ongoing since 1973.[3] A Delhi Transport Undertaking bus conductor allegedly charged 15 paise instead of 10 paise for a ticket. For the offence of pocketing 5 paise, Ranvir Singh Yadav

---

[3]Ketki Angre; 'He Was Sacked Over 5 Paisa; Legal Battle On For 40 Years'; NDTV.com; https://www.ndtv.com/delhi-news/delhi-bus-conductor-sacked-over-5-paisa-legal-battle-on-for-40-years-1402883
Accessed on 7 May, 2019

was terminated. The case was last posted for hearing in the Karkardooma Courts, Delhi, on 26 May 2016! In UP, two women were allegedly raped in 1989. The case has meandered, and continues to do so, even though one of the women and one of the accused have both already died!

While there may well be a case for having more judges and judicial infrastructure, the citizen wonders if enough judges will ever be available to decide upon the dispute between a leading Bollywood actor and his rumoured lady love, on whether Mumbai should have dahi handi during Janmashtami, or on how Mumbai bar girls should behave while dancing!

FIXING ACCOUNTABILITY FOR BROKEN WINDOWS

It would not be an exaggeration to state bluntly that the citizen feels absolutely disgusted by the state of affairs. Who is in charge? Where does the buck stop: central government, state government or the judiciary? In the five years of UPA-2 and the last two years of the NDA governments, the Union Law Ministry has had one new minister every year. The same has been the case with the CJI. The obsession of the government and the judiciary seems to be restricted to the appointment of new judges.

Even the media does not seem to comprehend the role it can play. The media spends hours of airtime and several units of blood pressure on whether Fawad and Mahira Khan must act in Hindi films or whether the Board of Control for Cricket in India (BCCI) should be better behaved with respect to the Lodha Committee report. How long has it been since you heard a national news hour debate on the justice delivery system?

All this leaves the common citizen bewildered and susceptible to the 'Broken Window' syndrome.[4] It is essentially a criminological theory that avers that if people see a broken window in a public building, they all assume that somebody is fixing the window, whereas the reality is that absolutely nobody is doing it. Fixing accountability for the broken windows is essential to secure order in society. Maintaining and monitoring urban environments to prevent small crimes such as vandalism and public drinking helps to create an atmosphere of order and lawfulness, thus preventing serious crimes from happening. Otherwise, the citizen's dilemma becomes, 'Nobody seems to care, so why should I bother?' In fact, lawyers Prashant Bhushan and Ravindra Badgaiyan have gone so far as to argue, 'Judicial ineffectiveness is *to a great extent* (emphasis mine) responsible for the increase in crimes like rape, murder, looting, cheating and so on.'[5]

---

[4]George Kelling and Catherine Coles; *Fixing Broken Windows: Restoring Order And Reducing Crime In Our Communities*; Free Press (1998)
[5]Prashant Bhushan, Ravindra Badgaiyan; 'Justice eludes'; *The Indian Express*; 20 Sep, 2016; https://indianexpress.com/article/opinion/columns/judiciary-justice-civilised-society-constitution-current-judicial-system-3039594/ Accessed on 18 April, 2019

Whether these comments are valid or not, we must consider this situation to be a great threat to public morality, democracy and justice in the future. It is difficult to fathom the lack of outrage on this subject among politicians, administrators, chambers of commerce, media and NGOs, all of whom demonstrate great capacity for agitation when it comes to other issues.

The citizen feels that although new rights like Right to Information (RTI) and Right to Education (RTE) are published and publicized periodically, there is no real progress towards ensuring Right to Justice, as assured in the Constitution of India. Logically, legal reform and actions should not create any controversy among political parties, so political consensus should not be a problem—at least, in the naïve view of the citizen. Regrettably, it has become so blasé, that legal reform wins no votes or eyeballs. Judicial reform has never been a poll promise. Reform of our justice system is important to all, but not important enough for anybody in particular!

JUSTICE, DEMOCRACY AND MORALITY

Threat to constitutional democracy

An inefficient justice delivery system would ultimately undermine and erode the citizens' faith in basic tenets of constitutional democracy. When Ajmal Kasab was arrested after the Mumbai terror attacks, many demanded that he should just be killed, and argued that a trial would be unnecessary. This is a dangerous sign, although not surprising—given the way cases linger on in our courts. But this is the consequence we need to be worried about. The day this country starts punishing without trial, we will cease to be a rule-of-law based society.

The same holds true for the hit-and-run case involving Salman. There was a great deal of outcry when he was granted bail on the same day as his conviction. In any fair criminal justice system, the right of first appeal against conviction should be given to an accused. There was nothing wrong in him getting bail while his appeal was being decided. But this becomes unacceptable to the general public when they are aware that the trial and conviction took more than a decade! Because of judicial delays, one starts questioning even the basic principles of criminal law.

Outrage can be used to motivate public reasoning

In the month that my mother delivered me into this world at Calcutta (December 1945), the British Famine Inquiry Commission reported on the Bengal Famine. It stated that the weekly death toll due to famine was then estimated at 26,000—far in excess of the colonial government's earlier estimate of 1,000 deaths per week. There was outrage, but not in the sense and the intensity that one would experience in a vibrant democracy. Fortunately, the condition of public outrage has since changed in our energetic democracy.

Recall the heightened expression of outrage and the public indignation after the Nirbhaya incident, an attribute that is considered a fundamental feature of democracy. In the words of Professor Amartya Sen, 'inflamed minds' can guide public policy to eliminate the occurence of similar injustices in the future. That this corrective step does not happen in India is a malfunctioning of democracy, carrying with it the message that as a nation, we need to fix the defect rather than merely be cynical about its existence.

We use the phrase 'justice should be done and should be seen to have been done.' Is there any connection between legal correctness and popular opinion? The origin of the expression dates back to 1923 when Lord Hewart of Bury, Lord Chief Justice of England, said words to this effect in a particular case. Why is this important? The fact of the matter is that it is easier to implement judgements that are generally acceptable in the court of public opinion. As Professor Sen has argued, 'There is a connection between the objectivity of a judgement and its ability to withstand public scrutiny.'

Of course, there will always be judgements with which some people would not agree. It happens all over the world. In October 2016, *The Times of India* reported that the District Mahila Court, Coimbatore, convicted a sixty-year-old man to five years' rigorous imprisonment for sexually assaulting a ten-year-old schoolgirl.[6] On the same day, it was reported

---

[6]Senthil Kumaran; '60-yr-old gets 5 years' RI for assaulting minor sexually'; *The Times of India*; 24 Oct, 2016

that a Fresno Superior Court in California handed out a sentence of 1503 years to a forty-one-year-old man who repeatedly raped his teenage daughter.[7] A few days earlier, *The New York Times* reported that a Montana judge in the US sentenced a man who repeatedly raped his own twelve-year-old daughter to just sixty days in jail.[8] As you would expect, the Montana judgement created a huge uproar among the public because justice was not perceived to have been done.

Whatever the merits of those cases, the fact that the justice system in the US was able to conclude speedily the cases pertaining to, for example, Goldman Sachs director Rajat Gupta or New York assembly speaker, Sheldon Silver, does strengthen public reasoning, the rule of law and the democratic framework. It is this structure that is ever so valuable in India, and that stands threatened with a loose and inefficient judicial system.

---

http://timesofindia.indiatimes.com/articleshow/55005226.cms?utm_source=contentofinterest&utm_medium=text&utm_campaign=cppst
Accessed on 18 April, 2019

[7]'Man sentenced to 1,503 years in prison for repeatedly raping his daughter'; *Fox News*; 24 Oct, 2016; https://www.foxnews.com/world/man-sentenced-to-1503-years-in-prison-for-repeatedly-raping-his-daughter
Accessed 18 April, 2019

[8]Niraj Chokshi; 'Outrage Follows 60-Day Sentence in Incest Case Against Father of Girl, 12'; *The New York Times*; 21 Oct, 2016; https://www.nytimes.com/2016/10/22/us/montana-judge-criticized-for-60-day-sentence-for-felony-incest.html
Accessed 18 April, 2019

Morality and effective legal systems

In his 1787 address to the British Parliament about the legal system, Edmund Burke had said, 'People crushed by law have no hopes from power. If laws are their enemies, they will be enemies to the laws; and those who have much to hope and nothing to lose will always be dangerous.'

An effective legal system can function if it is built on a strong moral foundation in society. When issues like Bofors, Commonwealth Games, 2G, and coal mines arise, there is vehement denial from the people accused. A long wait follows as the courts churn and twist through lies and facts. When the Panama leaks were reported, South Asians denied everything, whereas the Prime Ministers of Iceland and Britain accepted it and explained the facts.

Leaders should not and cannot lead by resorting only to the courts of law. The court of public opinion matters; it has a pervasive influence on perception. This reality should influence the behaviour of all leaders—companies, institutions and nations. Public opinion bestows the moral authority to lead when conduct and intent are perceived to be of a high standard.

Public perception demands more than self-esteem. Public perception is influenced by the four estates of democracy—the results achieved by the executive, the behaviour of legislators, the performance of the legal system and the projection of matters by the media. Our system seems to rely excessively on the media and the judiciary.

When it comes to the judiciary, all sorts of matters are referred to the already over-burdened courts: Bollywood squabbles over personal rivalries, which words affirm nationalism, whether women can enter a place of worship, cricket administrators' egoistic displays of fancy and power, and businessmen's larger-than-life personal activities. If the courts do decide (as in the case of IPL matches), critics say that there has been judicial over-reach. If they don't (as in the LGBT issue), then the courts are accused of not stretching themselves.

Public credulity is offended when a person in power behaves without the moral authority of leadership as Indians have seen during the course of the 2019 election campaigns.

If leaders without moral authority expect to lead their followers effectively, they are no leaders. The challenge is not only within our companies, political parties and governments, but also within clubs, gymkhanas, building societies and NGOs.

The collaborative leader needs to step back from the warlike posturing demanded by politics and be vulnerable. The methods were so well exemplified by Mahatma Gandhi, Nelson Mandela and Patricio Aylwin. As *The New York Times* columnist Roger Cohen has pointed out, 'Liberalism demands acceptance of our human differences and the ability to mediate them through democratic institutions… Liberalism may appear to be feeble as a battle cry, but nothing is more important for human dignity and decency.'

So what is the solution? As a common citizen, I feel hesitant to suggest solutions, especially when they can be found buried among numerous reports already with the government. Expert bodies seem to think that a solution lies at the intersection of:

i. More effective deployment of the budgetary provisions at the State and Centre.
ii. More efficient judicial procedures by shifting the focus from procedural issues to substantive issues.
iii. Limiting the number of adjournments sought by lawyers.
iv. More punitive measures against indulgences of a frivolous nature.
v. The judiciary judging itself and reforming.

I hope that our leaders recognize the gravity of the issue facing our young democracy and feel sufficiently motivated to launch a 'Swachh Insaaf' initiative. Certainly for business and enterprise, quick disposal of commercial disputes is a key part of 'ease of doing business'.

9

Resetting India's Mindsets

We have seen how India, as a young democracy, continues to grapple with challenges as diverse as agrarian distress and judicial delays. But have those issues impacted the way a majority of Indians perceive the country's future growth prospects? Do they believe that as the country transforms, some of its most persistent problems are likely to become weights that will slow its rise on the world stage? Or, do they think that one of the only two developing countries to score in the top ten in A.T. Kearney's Foreign Direct Investment Confidence Index—the other being China—is 'chaotic' but 'competitive'?[1]

---

[1]Salvatore Babones; 'India May Be The World's Fastest Growing Economy, But Regional Disparity Is A Serious Challenge'; *Forbes*; https://www.forbes.com/sites/salvatorebabones/2018/01/10/india-may-be-the-worlds-fastest-growing-economy-but-regional-disparity-is-a-serious-challenge/#1f70e4f753ac Accessed on 25 April, 2019

Through a survey among thinking people in 2010, I sought a response, to the statement, 'What is the probability that India will experience the best economic progress in the next fifteen years?' The most common answer was—hold your breath—80 per cent! Not one person pegged it at less than 70 per cent. The somewhat depressing signals reported in the media every morning in 2010 could not have warranted such a level of optimism.

To understand this upward trajectory, we must take a longer term perspective. I am no astrologer, though I have been accused of being an incurable optimist. Let us first reflect on the quiet economic revolutions around us. For instance, in the fields of communication and personal transportation, we have gone from zero to a billion cell phones in use, almost none to 100 million PCs, and 22 million to 100 million registered two wheelers, all in the last fifteen years. Rural employment too has been transformed: the rural non-agricultural employment (RNAE) annual growth rate doubled from 2.7 per cent in the 1990s to 5.3 per cent in the 2000s. With the passing of the distinguished Raj Krishna, the 'Hindu rate of growth' has also passed. It is really exciting that India is set to break into a game-changing trajectory. I hope to be around in 2025 to see if I am right.

NEW LOCOMOTIVES

So what is fuelling this leap into the future? For two centuries, the engines pulling the global economy have been

Europe and America. These engines are sputtering and are unable to pull the current increased load of bogies. The global financial system is frighteningly fragile. The developed nations are in far too much debt. As expert commentators continue to warn periodically, the economic crisis of 2008 has not evaporated. Further, developed nations can afford neither to continue nor to discontinue the stimulus. They are caught between the Scylla of joblessness and the Charybdis of indebtedness.

That is why the global economy needs new locomotives. David Rhodes and Daniel Stelter of Boston Consulting Group (BCG) report that the world will be a two-speed world with America, Europe, Japan and Russia experiencing a 'structurally subdued growth' while India, China and Brazil will 'soon approach their original trend-growth paths.'

However, I have a different view of India's evolving growth story, and would like to present a professional manager's perspective. Managers are deeply interested in the contexts of issues and their influence on the managerial mindset. Nobel Prize winner Daniel Kahneman had studied the fuzzy way in which people, in their daily economic lives, perceive things. Mine is an attempt in the same direction. It is flawed in its own way, but hopefully, it is different from the more common viewpoints encountered.

In management-speak, the term *strategic intent* is used to connote three dimensions—a sense of destiny, direction and discovery.[2] Simply put, this means that to truly understand the depth and direction of progress, one needs to appreciate the changes in mindset, because that is what precedes agendas and actions. As India undergoes a tremendous experiment in economic and social development, I would like to understand the mindset at three inflection points in the last seven decades of India's incredible journey.

MINDSET CHALLENGES ARISING FROM COLONIALISM

In 1930, Will Durant, speaking about India, noted that 'the economic drain out of resources of the land...has reduced India to a land of famines more frequent, more widespread and more fatal, than any known before in the history of India or of the world.'[3] Not surprisingly, the priority of dealing with food shortage was fully grasped only at the time of Independence in 1947. At that time, Amartya Sen's thesis was not known—that no substantial famine has ever occurred in any independent country with a democratic form of government and a relatively free press.[4] However, it is entirely correct to state that during the last seven decades of Independence, the exercise of political rights by the people of India has put pressure on the government, compelling

---

[2]Gary Hamel and CK Prahalad; Competing for the Future; Harvard Business Review Press
[3]Will Durant; The case for India; Simon and Schuster(1930)
[4]P.N. Dhar; The Evolution of Economic Policy in India: Selected Essays; Oxford University Press

it to respond to the acute suffering of the people. Potential famines have been prevented in India, often by creating countervailing employment.

It would be incorrect to derive the impression that avoidance of famine has been India's major achievement. The purpose of recounting the background in such an elaborate manner is to illustrate how the mindset of a nation can be shaped by its experiences.

In the course of the freedom struggle, a nationalist economic platform had emerged in the country.[5] The leadership was acutely aware of the need for industrialization to modernize the economy. The problem that some other countries faced was avoided—first, inadequate growth of food production and second, a lack of general economic growth due to an undiversified production structure. The nationalist economic agenda worked—imperfectly, but pragmatically.

MINDSET THAT REDEFINES THE PRODUCTIVITY SURGE

After Independence, the country had little foreign exchange and not much industrialization, and was in search of an appropriate development strategy. In those days, all intellectuals were in awe of socialism, and so was Nehru,

---

[5]'India's shining hopes'; *The Economist*; 21 Feb, 2004; https://www.economist.com/special-report/2004/02/19/indias-shining-hopes Accessed on 25 April, 2019

who was deeply impressed by his visit to the Soviet Union. The nation embarked on a centrally planned, socialist model of development, fortunately co-existing with private enterprise. Unfortunately, the results were not good enough. In most peoples' reckoning, 1991 was the year when liberalization began. Intuitionally, however, I have always felt that liberalization in India began in the 1980s with Mrs Indira Gandhi. The firmly shut door was eased open in 1981, but swung wide open later in 1991. She had probably felt scarred and battered by the experiences of economic controls and the planned economy, which she witnessed and participated in.

The long-term growth in India accelerated from 3.5 per cent in the 70s to 5.4 per cent in the 80s and 5.9 per cent in the 90s. Expressed more dramatically, it took fifty-seven years to double per capita GDP in the 1970s—now it takes only eighteen.[6] Due to the reduction of population growth, the per capita GDP has more than trebled from 1.2 per cent in the 70s to 3.9 per cent in the 90s. This clearly demonstrates that the transition to high growth occurred around 1980, a full decade before the 1991 liberalization, to which much credit (and criticism) accrues.

Dani Rodrik and Arvind Subramanian argued that the growth transition of the early 1980s was grounded in an

---

[6]Kelkar, Vijay L., and Sameer Kochhar. *India on the Growth Turnpike: Essays in Honour of Vijay L. Kelkar*. Academic Foundation, 2011.

impressive increase in productivity.[7] Amazingly, the total factor productivity in the period 1980–1999 surpasses that of even East Asia in the first twenty years of the East Asian miracle. So what caused this sudden jump in economic growth and productivity? Through their analysis, they ruled out factors such as external and internal liberalization, public investment and green revolution. They explained the transition through certain elements: first, an attitudinal change on the part of the government; second, the shift being pro-business rather than pro-competition; and third, the small shifts eliciting large productivity responses, because the Indian economy was operating well below its potential. Lastly, the already developed infrastructure for manufacturing played a key role in the growth, due to the stimulation of these factors.

I feel persuaded by the argument that there was a mindset change around 1980. Just as there was a pre-Independence mindset fashioned by the legacies of colonialism, there was an inflection in 1980, fashioned by the legacies of over thirty years of a centrally planned economy. My view is influenced by the comments—which I should not disclose here—that I heard from a non-executive director of HUL, M. Narasimham, who had served in key positions during Mrs Gandhi's second stint as Prime Minister in the early 1980s.

---

[7]Dani Rodrik & Arvind Subramanian; 'From "Hindu Growth" to Productivity Surge: The Mystery of the Indian Growth Transition'; NBER Working Paper No. 10376 Issued in March 2004

ACCELERATORS OF GROWTH

However, beyond the mindset change, it is also important to understand that India has some accelerators going for it.

Firstly, it is now a $2.5 trillion economy which is set to double every seven-eight years. India needs a couple of points more to accelerate economic progress.

Secondly, consumption expenditure constitutes an impressive percentage within India's GDP. When the per capita GDP, in Purchasing Power Parity (PPP) terms, moves above $3500, the demand for all sorts of goods and services takes off: food, eating out, personal transportation, housing and so on. And we are experiencing such consumption already. In the next fifteen years, India's per capita GDP in PPP terms will move up from the current level of about $3000. This was the starting level before the great American growth of the 1950s and 1960s. So the tipping point is within sight.

Thirdly, India's connectedness with the global economy is good, but not risky. India's import-export trade or dependence on foreign capital is less aggressive than China's.

Fourthly, India will reap the advantage of the demographic dividend. Europe reduced the replacement fertility rate from five to two over 130 years; Korea did so in twenty years; India will do so only by 2030.

Albeit in a meandering way, Indian economic policies have promoted productivity, renewal and globalization among Indian firms. If you compare the rankings of top companies in 1990 and today, the survival rate is only 20-25 per cent. Yesterday's giants like Escorts, Spic, and Modi Rubber have dropped off the charts. Today's giants like Bharti, Wipro and Infosys were barely noticeable in 1990.

Aside from the economic factors, there are political factors at play. No country in the world has wilfully adopted democracy ahead of capitalism and constitutional liberalism. This contrarian act is akin to climbing up on the 'down' escalator! India's journey does look confusing, but the direction is surely upwards. Of course, Indian democracy has huge fault lines: caste politics, the demand for more states, agitation for regional employment, tribal uprisings and so on. But do recall that at the equivalent stage of democratic evolution, the USA had a civil war! India has matured with respect to coalition politics. The previous UPA government lasted a full term with clear goals and accomplishments.

Dr S. Radhakrishnan had said, 'Tolerance is the homage which the finite mind pays to the inexhaustibility of the Infinite.' These positive social factors have played an important role in India's growth story. Recall that since the unfortunate Gujarat riots of 2002, there has been no major communal trouble in the country. Religious diversity is an accepted character of Indian society. Slightly under half of the daily 10,000 pilgrims to the Khwaja Moinuddin Chishti's dargah at Ajmer are non-Muslims. Leaving aside the controversy about women entering the temple, the Ayyappa temple at Sabarimala is thronged not only by Hindus, but also by Muslims and Christians like singer Yesudas, who was inspired by Sabarimala. The Wednesday Novena at St Michael Church, Mahim, is routinely thronged by non-Christians. Although not in our consciousness, religious and social harmony promotes business. History shows this to be the case. India's economic progress receives a boost from the nation's openness and its ability to communicate and work with other cultures.

GOVERNMENT FOCUS ON SOCIAL INFRASTRUCTURE

These accelerators alone will hardly be enough to deliver the change that young India demands and deserves. In this quest to achieve shared prosperity for its burgeoning population, the government has a very important role to play. It must partner with the corporate world to implement new developmental approaches. The action agendas on 'direct' economic determinants like industry, energy and infrastructure automatically get the attention of the government and the chambers of commerce. But what about a wish list of 'indirect' determinants or drivers which an entrepreneurial private sector cannot accomodate on its own, and hence the government needs to uniquely act upon?

Yes, I would say 'better governance' in short. My list would be as follows:

- Health: provide safe drinking water and health care

- Education: overhaul primary education and skill development
- Law: address the injustice of delayed justice
- Pakistan: find a way to coexist with the neighbour

These citizen issues need greater and more urgent focus in government.

ENTREPRENEURIAL MINDSET DRIVES THE AGENDA

After several years of the deregulation mindset, there is an entrepreneurial mindset driving the agenda for the foreseeable future. Unlike the generations before them, young Indians are no longer obsessed with India's poverty, but with its future. This gives India a fighting chance. When I look around I believe that entrepreneurship has always been in the national gene, and that the openness to productivity ideas has been a strong driver.

So is this enterprise a creative and innovative response to the environment? David McClelland established the now widely accepted view that enterprise is promoted by a high achievement orientation, which can in turn be promoted by enriching people's thoughts and fantasies with the language of achievment. Four factors influence entrepreneurship. First, the experiences that an individual undergoes, which impact his attitude to enterprise; second, the traditions of the family and society in which he lives; third, the support systems of finance and vocational training/extension services which equip him to become entrepreneurial; and fourth and last, the governmental policy framework, which needs to be supportive and mentoring.

ENTREPRENEURS CREATE A SPIRAL OF GROWTH

In addition to the above factors, I strongly believe that entrepreneurship is contagious and success attracts others in a virtuous cycle—a cycle in which India is now happily placed. Let's compare the concept of entrepreneurship to the zillions of frenetic atoms in apparently stable and solid matter. What is perceived as solid matter, as physicists will tell you, is actually vast amounts of empty space, interspersed with tiny constituents called atoms. Although the earth that we stand on feels solid, in reality, it is zillions of atoms separated by small spaces. Such is the case with everything around us, including the human body. Thus a microscopic view of the human body would render it a collection of numerous atoms, buzzing with energy and in constant interaction with each other.

We are not as solid as we think! The thought is sobering, and although it borders on the metaphysical and spiritual, it gives us great insight into the potential of human beings. We are nothing but an assortment of zillions of packets of energy—zillions of buzzing and constantly moving atoms.

Imagine how wonderful it would be if this enormous amount of energy could be channelized. Atomic science has shown that when certain atoms, like those of uranium, are hit by neutrons, they split and release further neutrons which split other uranium atoms, causing a self-sustaining reaction. This results in an incredible amount of energy being unleashed.

If we extend this analogy, we realize that we are 1.3 billion people, who are, in turn, composed of zillions of highly energetic atoms. Imagine the energy that can be unleashed if there is a chain reaction in this conglomeration.

History is replete with testimonies to human enterprise creating self-sustaining spirals of growth. What is really fascinating is to discover that Indians have always been at the forefront of exploiting this inherent entrepreneurial flair. An enterprising community is characterized by an outward-looking attitude and a willingness to explore new ideas as well as to accept exogenous influences. These characteristics have been vibrant in our history through the centuries. Right from ancient times until 1900, India had been entrepreneurial and had a foreign trade surplus. As late as the 1920s, India was ranked fourth in world trade with a market share of 2.5 per cent (as against 0.7 per cent today). Trading took Indians to Africa, the Caribbean, Malaysia and the Arab world over the centuries. Therefore the central planning and socialist policies during the first few decades of independent India frustrated the natural entrepreneur, but failed to supress him. That centuries-old DNA of entrepreneurship and restlessness has once again started to find release—that is why Indian businessmen are again in a mood to go out and do business both in India and with the rest of the world.

Look at the phenomenal transformation of Gurugram (or Gurgaon). What started off as a sluggish little city now has an annual industrial sector turnover of strategic importance. There are many prominent and prestigious units involved in the manufacturing or development of automobiles, telecommunication equipment, electrical goods, software, hardware, sports goods, etc. The employment generated in the industrial sector exceeded 200,000 persons around 2017.

Going across the Vindhyas, we can only marvel at the way the entrepreneurial drive has transformed the sleepy Sriperumbudur corridor. From the early 2000s till date, the town has undergone a sea change, with hosts of multinationals like Hyundai, Saint-Gobain, Ford, Hindustan Motors, Mitsubishi, BMW and Nissan setting-up operations, turning this Chennai suburban town into a large-scale industrial hub.

The existing car production capacity in the Sriperumbudur-Chennai belt itself translated into employment of approximately 500,000 people around 2017. This has created a huge multiplier effect of tertiary employment for millions who supply these salaried employees with food, clothing, shelter, education, medical facilities and entertainment. A significant number of these people are first time vendors/entrepreneurs who are participating in, and co-creating, this ecosystem of opportunities. Entrepreneurship is inherent in human nature and has the potential to create a spiral of growth, much like the unleashing of tremendous energy when atoms are subjected to stimulating conditions.

I believe a very strong instrumentality for this growth has been the adoption of productivity techniques, as admitted by companies like Tata Steel and TVS. For instance, until the 1980s, one would not find global consultants operating in India. Today, you would find McKinsey, BCG, A.T. Kearney, Accenture and several others, serving clients who are hungry to cut costs, improve margins and become competitive.

In terms of quality, after years of effort by chambers of commerce, companies have adopted world-class quality as an essential part of strategy. The first time any Indian company got the Deming Prize was in 1998, but that was followed by one in 2001, two in 2002 and five in 2003. Similarly, Indian companies have been felicitated with the TPM Excellence Award—one each in 1995, 1998 and 1999, followed by three in 2000, seven in 2001, eight in 2002 and fourteen in 2003. Of all the software firms in the world certified at the highest level of CMM, level 5, three-fourths are in India! So, for sure, one can recognize some of the instrumentalities that have been responsible for the changes that are occurring.

Entrepreneurial behaviour is contagious and creates a flock mentality—a bit like gold prospecting.[8] Idea entrepreneurs

---

[8]C.B. Schoonhoven & E. Romanelli (Eds), *The Entrepreneurship Dynamic: Origins of Entrepreneurship and the Evolution of Industry*; Stanford University Press

in knowledge industries create new ideas, new segments or entirely new markets. Thus, it was Texas Instruments which first set up a global research and development (R&D) centre in Bangalore twenty years ago. Several others flocked there and today there are a hundred global R&D centres in Bangalore. Prior to 1995, venture capitalism was unknown in India. Venture investment in India in 1996-97 was $20 million—whereas in recent years, it has reached $6 billion! Thus, there has been a mindset change among venture capitalists (VCs) as well as entrepreneurs.

Let me now illustrate this entrepreneurship through three anecdotal examples of manufacturing, knowledge and microfinance.

MANUFACTURING: MOUNTING A CHALLENGE TO CHINA

Just a few years ago, the constant refrain of the Indian industry to the government was that multinational corporations (MNCs) would dominate and protection was essential. In December 2003, the Finance Minister dropped the effective import duty by 5 percentage points. Between April 2003 and March 2004, the rupee *appreciated* by 9 percentage points whereas Indians have had fifty years' experience with devaluation. Both were noticed, but that was about it. Indian industry went ahead with attending to its agenda, rather than cribbing or complaining. Between November 2003 and April 2004, Indian companies acquired forty-four companies abroad, worth $2 billion.[9]

There is also something happening out there in manufacturing. Moser-Baer, a firm near Delhi, is one of the world's largest optical media manufacturers, and one of the lowest cost producers of CD-recorders. Its exports are over a quarter of a billion dollars! Hero MotoCorp is the world's largest two-wheeler company by volume. Essel Propack is the world's largest manufacturer of laminated plastic tubes, with units operating across countries such as the US, Mexico, Colombia, Poland, Germany, UK, Egypt, Russia, China and Philippines. Tata Steel is still in the global top five in terms of the cost of making hot-rolled coil.

A NEW JOURNEY IN R&D

India has a long tradition of knowledge. The world's first university was established in Takshila in 700 BC. The value of pi was calculated in India, as also the invention of quadratic equations. Today, there are 400 engineering colleges producing 350,000 out of a world output of 900,000 engineers per annum. We have over 2000 management schools, which turn out about 100,000 management graduates—roughly similar to the US and much more than, say, Britain or Germany. Admittedly, the quality varies greatly, but the best are truly outstanding. The list of multi nationals setting up R&D

---

[9]Arun Shourie; 'Charge of the Indian Brigade'; *Indian Express*
Arun Shourie; 'Listen to the New India', *Indian Express*

centres in India includes General Electric, Microsoft, IBM, Cisco, Intel, Astra Zeneca, Motorola and Texas Instruments.[10] Patent applications in India have shot up from 4,000 in 1995 to 20,000 now. The Indian subsidiary of Intel filed for several patents, engaging 1500 professionals at its R&D centre in Bangalore in 'engineering challenges as complex as any other project on the planet.' Inadvertently, I should not give the impression that India alone has captured the world's intellect to the detriment of other countries. We have well and truly set out on a new journey in R&D. Sarnoff, an American R&D firm, has correctly argued that of the three requirements for developing an innovation-driven industry, India has two: the technical skills and access to capital. What is missing is an indigenous business model.

So why are foreign companies, some of whom have budgets higher than India's R&D budgets, moving their R&D, in part, to India? There are several reasons. First, the cost of doing R&D here is a fraction of that in the developed world. Second, there is a pretty robust technical educational system, producing some excellent manpower. Third, foreign companies are seeking access to high quality engineers due to problems of availability or cost in their home countries. Fourth, R&D globally has become multi-geographic with innovation-specific patterns of collaboration and diffusion. This has allowed GE to set up the John F.

---

[10] R.A. Mashelkar; 'From Brain Drain to Brain Gain'; Convocation Address at Pune University, 26 December 2000

Welch Technology Center (JFWTC) at Bangalore with over a couple of thousand engineers, engaged in fundamental research for most of GE's thirteen divisions.

Knowledge is a strong entrepreneurial force in India.

MICROFINANCE: FINANCIAL INCLUSION TO THE NEXT LEVEL

It is not just about entrepreneurship being unleashed through manufacturing and knowledge. Ideas are being generated and experimented with in the most potent area of rural entrepreneurship, through microfinance. A scalable and high impact model is still elusive, though a number of experiments are ongoing.

Microfinance concerns the small loans given to the poor by NGOs to help start small businesses. The world over, microfinance is synonymous with Grameen Bank, Bangladesh. In India, too, a few organized entities like SHARE Microfin and SKS (now Bharat Financial Inclusion Limited) had pioneered microfinance initiatives in backward areas of the country, including tribal areas. An Indian-born venture capital specialist from Silicon Valley and a Berkeley professor, Vinod Khosla and Atanu Dey, had conceptualized Rural Infrastructure Services for Commons (RISC), a sort of Marshall Plan for the reconstruction of rural India. They maintained that $1 million would be enough to provide power, telecom, transportation and financial infrastructures to 100,000 rural people. Hence, with $5 billion, one could create the infrastructure to liberate 500 million rural people. The village or community society would receive the investment directly on behalf of its 100,000 members. Entrepreneurs in that village society would receive their loans directly based on a business plan. The founders felt that even if the economic output was raised by only 10 per cent, the project would pay back for itself. Of course, this was only an idea, but it seems that it never took off!

CELEBRATING THE TRUE SPIRIT OF INDIAN ENTREPRENEURSHIP

Nothing celebrates the spirit behind every entrepreneurial act like the following incident, which happened during military manoeuvres in Switzerland. A young lieutenant sent his recce unit into the icy wilderness of the Alps. Unexpectedly, it started to snow for two whole days and the recce unit did not return. The lieutenant was very upset, thinking that he had been foolish in his leadership. On the third day, the unit returned safely, miraculously. What happened?

Well, they were truly lost and they were sure their end was near. They pitched camp, and then suddenly one person found a map in his pocket. Using the map, they found their way out. The lieutenant asked to see the map. To his astonishment, it was not a map of the Alps, but of the Pyrenees.

It would appear that when you are lost, any old map will do. That is at the heart of entrepreneurship, in which self-confidence is a strategy in itself. When a leader treats a vague map as if it had some meaning, meaning is automatically produced. With that shred of meaning, he initiates action. The action makes it possible to learn what is going on and to initiate the next action. After all, you only learn by doing things, not by planning for the perfect actions. But the greatest secret of any form of entrepreneurship is that optimism is not a denial of reality; indeed, it is that very optimism that makes the reality possible.

This most valuable gene of Indian enterprise has prospered, through invasions, battles and colonialism. It is firmly embedded in the Indian gene. It has required periodic refreshment, but has never had to be resurrected. This long-standing propensity for enterprise amongst Indians is a remarkable asset. Indian entrepreneurs must move ahead with their historical vigour.

The sheer adventure of India's economic growth, with social justice and entrepreneurship, is staggering. But this journey is not without pitfalls and challenges, like the high fiscal deficit of our government, the urgent need to take development programmes and jobs to rural areas, the inadequate state of our infrastructure, and so on. These are real problems awaiting solutions.

However, no comparable experiment of balancing growth, entrepreneurship and social justice has been undertaken in human history by any other developing country on such a large scale. To borrow from a generalization of Lord Keynes, one hopes that my country is likely to do the rational, since most alternatives have already been tried! In the next few decades, India has the real possibility to be once more at the top of the league tables among the nations of the world—a position she once held for centuries, but lost in the last few hundred years.

Most important, however, is the central goal of all development—ushering in change with a human face or 'insaaniyat', which means humaneness and nobility towards human beings. This is work-in-progress, and needs to be viewed in that perspective.

The coming decades will be truly momentous, as India's insaaniyat journey will continue to be scripted. No wonder, there is a palpable air of excitement in India and around the world.

10

Nation, Society and Business Enterprise

In this last chapter of this book, I shall ruminate about our nation, our society and the personal satisfactions that a career in business management and entrepreneurship can bring. I am not an anthropologist, sociologist, economist or historian, and, for sure, I lack the academic credentials in these subjects; that does not mean that I have not been touched by these subjects in the normal course of my half-a-century career in business management and entrepreneurship. What I have written in this essay is a pilgrim's account of the wonder that is India and the role of business enterprise in this wonderful nation of ours.

The scope of such a subject permits me to comment on all sorts of things, a bit like how a weekend golfer feels when he stands on a tee box with vast and broad fairways. However, the lessons of sports teach us that even while poised on such a tee box, the golfer must be disciplined and focused. I propose to make my comments and observations in four parts.

THE SOCIETY OF INDIA

I used to take our society for granted. I was born into it—and I thought that I knew it all too well. Over the years, I have come to realize that I have barely known India; it is all of what I know, but it is also a lot of what I do not know; what I know of India is my version—a very valid version—but there are many more versions, may be a lakh or a crore—really, nobody knows how many! The fact is that each of those versions is real for those who believe and inherit it. Therefore, one must be sensitive and careful while asserting what the true nature of the Indian nation is. This is a nation and society like no other on this planet. To me, that makes the Indian nation and society the first wonder of the world.

Every Indian needs to deeply understand this multi-level reality, and to never allow anybody, whether a politician, an administrator or an academic, to distract or interfere with the multiple versions of what India is. Understanding this idea of many Indias, appreciating the diversity and respecting alternative viewpoints is a key part of business. Every business enterprise seeks consumers for its company products and services. It becomes crucially important and basic for business folks to understand the multiple Indias.

This was finely captured by the approach advocated by Hindustan Unilever (HUL) when the company stated its aim as WIMI—Winning in many Indias.

As Tony Joseph mentions in the epilogue of his fascinating book, *Early Indians*, India can be defined as a 'multi-source civilization, which draws its cultural impulses and its practises from a variety of heredities and migration histories.' He also points to an academic paper that shows that the perception of India having a large population of 1.3 billion people is, genetically speaking, not quite correct. There are very few Indian groups that are demographically very large, and that the genetic difference among Indian groups is two to three times larger than the genetic difference between northern and southern Europeans. 'The truth is that India is composed of a large number of small populations.'

This is blindingly obvious to business folks. Yet, our society experiences stresses and challenges, painfully palpable in the public discourse, when self-styled leaders try to define an idea of India for all Indian people without conceding that there are alternate and valid views of India.

In the next few paragraphs, I will attempt to describe this multi-level reality—not to prove its existence, but to demonstrate its iridescence.

Weft and weave

One of India's oldest technologies and trades is in textiles. It can be traced back to the Indus Valley civilization. However, there are references to weaving in the Rig Veda, Ramayana and Mahabharata, predating even this period. Dilettantes of weaving and textiles traditions, like Suraiya Hasan Bose, have spent their lives trying to understand the complex weaving traditions of India.[1] These remarkable scholars of textile tradition deploy a painstaking technique of literally reverse-engineering the weft and the weave, by decoding available fragments of surviving textile pieces from old times. In this manner, they recreate the 'jaalas' or graphs that must have been used in those early times. Such a thrilling recreation of the past using techniques of reverse-engineering! Indian society is a lot like that. Questions that might interest someone like me—such as, who is a Tamil, who is a Tamil Brahmin, and where did they come from—can be adapted for a hundred different communities and groups within the country. The answers are not easy to get, but if they can be obtained and are assembled, you get a fabric showing how iridescent Indian society is.

I possess a book, in seven volumes, about the castes and tribes of Southern India. [2] It was authored by a former English Superintendent of Ethnography, who conducted his work in Southern India and published his findings as a book in 1909. It contains about two thousand words per caste/tribe and has listed over three hundred castes of southern India in

---

[1]Suvasisni Sridharan, 'Picking up lost threads with Suraiya Hasan Bose', *The Hindu* 5 May 2019
[2]*Castes and Tribes of Southern India*, Edgar Thurston and K Rangachari, 1909

alphabetical order. No wonder it took seven volumes, and, I must repeat, covered only southern India. I would not be far off the mark if I stated that India is not a homogenous group of 1.3 billion people—rather, it is a heterogenous agglomeration of three thousand castes and tribes, each caste or tribe having 400,000 people on an average! Indeed, during my penning of the social changes experienced by my ancestors, I have estimated that my community of Tamil Iyengar Brahmins may number only about 200,000 globally.[3] It is bewildering to an observer that even in the India of today, a large proportion of marriages (may be 60 per cent) are conducted within such community subsets, as evidenced to a degree by the matrimonial columns of the newspapers. Visit any matrimony website, and you can see the demand for grooms and brides, stratified and sub-stratified within the fine wafts and webs of Indian society.

The accuracy of my estimate is not the question. The right question to ask, and marvel about, is—how can 3,000 distinct communities, each comprising 400,000 people, live together in relative social harmony—not just today, but over centuries? Every religion of the world is practised in India, whether the Abrahamic trio or the indigenous quartet. For sure, it is not religion or language that binds Indian society together. So what is it that binds them together, while allowing them to maintain distinct identities? And to think that each community has its own perception of India

---

[3]*A comma in a sentence*, R. Gopalakrishnan, Rupa Publications, 2013

is to contemplate diversity that truly boggles the mind, like a fabric woven with a 'jaala' of incalculable beauty. Such diversity may well account for the stability of a people. It is just as much the reason why social tensions can easily be provoked by throwing matchsticks into the dry tinder.

I feel incredibly inspired and proud to recall the lines of Allama Mohammed Iqbal, who wrote in his celebrated poem, *'Taraana-e-Hindi',* in 1904:

> *Dharam aapas may dwesh nahin sikhaata, Hindi hain ham watan hai, Hindostan hamara,*
> *Yunan our Misr aur Rome, sab mit gaye hain, Ab tak magar hai baaki, naam aur nishaan hamara.*

Loosely translated, it means that religion does not teach enmity—we are all Indians and Hindustan is ours. China, Egypt and Rome have all lost their original civilizations, but ours still exists, not just in name, but also in practise.

The world's only colloidal society

One of my privileges has been to travel the length and breadth of our wonderful nation in the course of my professional duties. Yet, there are many unexplored places I have on my bucket list. While thinking about our people, I have sought inspiration from science and chemistry to explain our great macro-stability despite micro-level disequilibrium. And I think I found something interesting in my colloidal chemistry lessons from school.

If I take a spoonful of white salt and stir it into a glass of water, I will get a glass containing a homogenous solution. If I take a spoonful of sand and stir it into a glass of water, the sand will precipitate to the bottom, lying all by itself, distinct and visibly separate from the water. In chemistry, these states are called solution and precipitation.

If I stir a spoonful of white wheat-flour in a glass of white milk, something strange occurs. The wheat-flour does not dissolve, but neither does it precipitate. It disperses uniformly through the milk—visible and separate, yet homogenously dispersed throughout the milk. Further, the light reflected from this composite glass is no longer white, but bluish in color. In chemistry, this is called the Tyndall effect, named after the British scientist who explained the phenomenon as occurring due to the scattering of light.

Think about the societies all around the world. There are many societies, which comprise a hotchpotch of races and communities (mostly due to invasions). However, due to historical developments, they were homogenized to a great degree through social and political events such as eliminating the non-conformers—think of the Spanish Inquisition or the Catholic-Protestant divide. China has a homogenous society which is 95 per cent Han Chinese. Arabs are united, not politically, but by language and religion. Americans were once united by their common mission of a flight from misery. Although not homogenous, America is a young and complex society, but far simpler and more comprehensible than India. Europe succeeded in creating strong nation states in the 1800s through, for example, Garibaldi's integration of the Italian States or Bismarck's integration of the German State. Since then, these nation states have tried to integrate despite their diverse languages, religions and societies, but have faltered all the way through.

It is ironic that when India secured her freedom, British intellectuals and thinkers predicted a quick break-up, under the mistaken impression that the British had held undivided India together. Their judgement has been proven wrong, even though the history of independent India, as well as recent events, might give the impression that such an event might yet occur. The British Empire divided Ireland by religion, as they did Palestine and Cyprus. What they created was mayhem in each of these places. They did it again in India and left behind perhaps the biggest mayhem of them all. Britain's historical record of dividing the nations under their rule by religion must count as among the biggest epochal disasters through the twentieth century.

The central point about Indian society is that an idea of India has existed for millennia. It is true that it has not existed as a politically united nation for as long—at any rate, the idea of the nation state is a little older than a century. However, as Allama Iqbal pointed out, the practises and customs of Hindustani civilization from millennia ago are still recognizable in the way modern Indians live and practise religious and social relationships. This is stupendous and unmatched anywhere else in the world. It is a truism to state that India is a rare colloidal society in the world—arguably the world's only colloidal society!

Encounters with colloidal India

During my observations amidst work and travels, I have encountered and experienced the complex fabric of India as living proof of this colloidal India. I quote just five exotic examples, merely to illustrate that diversity and harmony is all around us Indians, but we do not necessarily notice these as oddities, since we see them every day.

i. Hussaini Brahmins are a Mohiyal community with ties to both Hindusim and Islam. The community got dispersed from Lahore in 1947 and now live in Sind, Rajasthan and Maharashtra. There is a community of some one hundred Hussaini Brahmin families living in Pune. They observe Hindu festivals, worship Shiva, and also observe Muharram. About fifteen hundred Husseini Brahmin families used to live in Baghdad around the time of the Battle of Karbala in 680 CE. They have surnames like Dutt and Mohan, though not everyone with those surnames is a Husseini Brahmin. The most notable member of this community was actor Sunil Dutt.

ii. The Siddis of Karnataka are a people descended from the Bantu tribes of south-east Africa, brought by Portuguese merchants to India several hundred years ago. As a young Area Sales Manager in Karnataka, I came across these Siddis in the areas around Haliyal and Ankola. I was amazed to encounter them: they spoke Kannada, looked like East Africans, followed their own customs, but also joined in on local customs—a perfect mélange. They were sometimes referred to as *habshi*, a derivative from the Al-Habsh, the Arabic word for what was Abyssinia or Ethiopia.

iii. The Parsis have been very close to my experiences— partly due to my professional career with Tata, and as a resident of Mumbai. The story of the wealthy and elite Parsis is too well known for me to recount here. The landing of the Zoroastrians, fleeing from religious persecution in their native Persia, in Gujarat can be traced back to the seventh century. This community is a living example of total integration into Indian society while maintaining a separate identity and customs. They are a cosmopolitan community in many ways. An early Indian Parsi who acquired enormous wealth was Jamsetjee Jeejebhoy, who made his money through the opium trade with China. Interestingly, he began his trading firm with a remarkable diversity of partners—Motichund Amichand, a Jain, Mohamad Ali Rogay, a Konkani Muslim, and Rogeiro de Faria, a Catholic from Goa.[4]

---

[4]Thomas Manuel, *'The opium trader who became one of India's richest men'*, *The Hindu*, 5 May 2019

iv. The Patnulkarar, or Saurashtrian Tamils, are Brahmins, originally from Saurashtra in Gujarat. After Mahmud of Ghazni desecrated the Somnath temple in their native Saurashtra, they migrated south in search of safer havens. The meaning of Pat-nul-karar in Tamil is 'silk-thread-person'. They were a community of silk thread merchants and weavers, so they built their new lives and relationships on that basis. They are immensely successful entrepreneurs who are part of the Tamil whole yet distinct in their identity.

v. Gadi Bero Tamils are Tamils who live in a village called Gadi Bero in Bengal. I became curious about this Tamil community in Bengal, because I am bilingual. Gadi Bero is a distortion, I was told, of Gaddi Veedu, which means the 'throne house'. The Tamil Gaddi Veedu became the Bengali Godi Bero over centuries. A Kanchipuram priest was recruited to serve the community under the regime of the Raja of Panchakot in the Purulia area of Bengal. He was given land to establish a temple and to earn a living. Around this event, traced to the times of Aurangzeb in Delhi, a community of Tamil Iyengars developed. Their dress and appearance is more authentic than their Mylapore equivalents, but they speak only Bengali, while observing Tamil Brahmin customs.

If I was a social anthropologist, I could have been more detailed in my commentaries and provided many more examples. But the reader has not purchased this book for social anthropology. I would hope that these five examples suffice to demonstrate the diversity, stability and harmony of the India that I took for granted as I grew up. Now I realize that this is most precious inheritance that must be nurtured by every Indian.

It is easy to lose it amidst the turmoil of increasing population and individual aspirations. After all, recall what happened in Germany within the last century. Adolf Hitler was appointed Chancellor of Germany in 1933. Within two months, the Nazi Party enacted The Enabling Act of 1933, which allowed Hitler's government to bypass Parliament and pass laws. Six years later, the Second World War ravaged the world, resulting in an anti-Semitic genocide. Such unstable-minded regimes can disturb the equilibrium of centuries-old, ecologically balanced societies.

SERVING SOCIETY IN INDIA

Every young person is, and should be, idealistic—wishing to serve the nation and society. There are many roles that can be performed in order to serve the nation. All of them have a distinct and value-adding aspect. Business management and entrepreneurship is one such role. Throughout my career, I have learnt that business enterprise can be a soul-elevating experience—it has been so for me!

Listening to left-leaning politicians, economists,

academics and journalists, one could conjure up a vision of greedy, power-hungry megalomaniacs as inhabitants of the mercantile world. It would not be an incorrect vision, but it would be a seriously partial one. It would be as true and valid as damning every profession and community through examples of the venal among them. I wish to share my own experiences and epiphanies gathered over half a century of my mercantile experience.

To use the metaphor of an automobile—good vehicles require one component that can burn an energy-rich fuel into mechanical power efficiently, that is, in an internal combustion engine. That is not all—the mechanical energy thus generated must provide maximum bang for the buck through efficiency and technology. A good vehicle must have a second component that transmits the mechanical energy to the rotating wheels through a gear and transmission. The third and last component of good vehicles is the handling and braking, which also encompasses the seating comfort of the passengers—who must experience both comfort and progress while in the car.

Likewise, in a society, there must, first, be an aggressive entrepreneurial bunch of people, because they are the combustible fuel that will drive the economy and growth. Second, this entrepreneurial energy must be guided with skill and rules of engagement through progressive measures in education, health, housing and communication. The third and last component is the equivalent of braking and handling—measures that will assure a minimum security from internal and external disturbances and threats, as well as justice and equality of opportunity. In commonly understood parlance, these three components of a wholesome society are Business, Infrastructure and Government.

I have learnt by applying this allegory that the primary energy generating activity in a society is business and entrepreneurship. I place business enterprise on a pedestal. If there were no petrol stations in a country, there would be no point in having Ferraris and Maseratis on the road. Business enterprises, in my humble view, should be as much on a pedestal as educationists, road-builders, administrators and the defence forces. I consider my career to have been devoted to the national good, no less than the best in defence or administration. My impact may have been less than another, but that has nothing to do with being in business or IAS or the army. When I hear young people say that they joined the IAS to do national service, I respect their view as much as I realize that there are many other ways to also deliver national service.

Upon reflection, I confess that I have been singularly fortunate to have served two great corporations, Unilever and Tata. My view that business can be a force for good in society springs from my experiences in these two companies. It goes to demonstrate the obvious—that good business can be conducted by good people with good results and for the national good. That is the bottom line. HUL has been India's 'most Indian' multinational corporation for decades, while Tata has been India's 'most multinational' Indian company for decades. Both have been highly ethical and responsible companies for a long time—over a century and a half—with occasional displays of the human frailties that all of us are prone to. In fact, it is those occasional frailties that remind the observer that there are no gods in society—there are some outstanding people and many good people, with a small number of misdirected people.

Indian businesses have for long displayed their own form of philanthropy. Merchant charity in India can be traced centuries back. Initially the activities were caste- or community-centric, like building temples, wells and schools in native villages. Lately, Indian philanthropy has widened to more modern forms. The great and exemplary work by charitable trusts established by Tata, Godrej, Birla, Bajaj and many others is a standing testimony to a responsive Indian tradition of charity and pursuing social good. Legislative innovations and business responsiveness, for example, the 2 per cent compulsory Corporate Social Responsibility (CSR), enhance and modernize traditional Indian philanthropy.

Occasionally; I hear comments that Indian business is less generous compared to other wealthy industrial nations. I doubt that this is true India is on a journey to be sure, where some others may be ahead. Like with many other things about India, there is catching-up to do, but there is no cause or room for cynical criticism or despair.

As some scholars have pointed out, society has three types of people, all operating in the same cauldron. There are 'the fearful', who are people with wealth and status but who are afraid of losing them swiftly. Think of zamindars and the princely states from before Independence; think of the wealthy, slow growth Japanese or European countries, who are anxious that their future generations may be worse off than their own. Then, there are 'the humiliated' who seek to establish themselves as equal members of society—a position that they have failed to achieve because of the historical malpractises of the privileged. Recall the tribal and Dalit communities in India, or the Arabs in the world economic order, as examples of the tormented. Lastly, there are 'the aspirants', the people who fight with industriousness and hard work to win a better life for themselves and their descendants. Think of the South Asian, Chinese and Indian economies. Just as the nurturing and support of the south eastern, Chinese and Indian economies has been important for the global economy, business and enterprise, the aspirant class in the Indian economy will get increasing and legitimate nurturing and support in the coming years.

Business and entrepreneurship can do what governments and infrastructures cannot. Business and trade alone can create wealth, growth and jobs. I feel optimistic that this distinctive role for business in the national economy will be supported by society in the emerging India. Business management is a great career for young people—for at least the next fifty years! As it so happens, Indian business comes with a great tradition of practise.

INDIAN ENTREPRENEURIAL TRADITION

Trade was built on specific competitive advantages—trust, domain knowledge, supply chains and information. Trust was an important competitive platform. Merchants were prominent members of society in the ancient Tamil country and were held in high esteem. The merchants of Poompuhar on the eastern coast (near modern-day Nagapattinam) were described in literature as being 'as straightforward as the crosspiece of a yoke...they value their goods and goods of others by the same standard...they openly state their profits...'[5] In the famous Sangam epic *Silappadikaram,* the central characters of the story belonged to one such eminent merchant family from Poompuhar.

The Tamilakam traders had great domain knowledge and were skilled and knowledgeable about assessing the commodities they dealt in. Based on the commodity, they organized themselves into guilds, as corroborated by the geographic distribution of inscriptions. Supply chain management was yet another competitive advantage. The Kutchis from Gujarat acquired a deep understanding of ship-building and navigational techniques. They were able to leverage wind patterns, ocean currents and the stars above

---

[5] Kanakalatha Mukund, *The Merchants of Tamilakam*, Penguin, 2012.

more skilfully than any other Indian trader. These enabled them to trade with Oman, Zanzibar and East Africa.

Information, both explicit and implicit, was the final competitive advantage. Mandvi on the Gujarat coast became a market city, somewhat like what Dubai has become in modern times, and was teeming with Arab and African traders apart from the local Kutchis. The Mandvi merchants possessed information on every local market, whether in India, Oman or Zanzibar, and their expertise enabled them to succeed in each of those markets.

On the western coast of India, just north of modern-day Kochi, there used to be a thriving port called Muziris. A papyrus scroll in the Vienna Museum dating to around 100 CE has a contract written in Greek between two merchants, one in Muziris and another in Alexandria. There is other evidence of written contracts, covering the duration of the voyage, the quantities and value of the goods traded, and finally, the terms of payment.

Multan, in the north-western part of the country, was a thriving trade centre. Here, traders from different countries in Central Asia and Persia came to trade with Indians. The Multani Indians were perceived to be particularly successful, and their success was attributed to their commercial structures. They mastered the technical skills to conduct long-distance trade relations and designed a fully integrated commercial structure, comprised of local agents and dispute resolution representatives all over north India. The family-run firm was at the heart of their system, but to run a far-flung business, they developed systems of senior and ordinary agents all over their territories of interest.

Poompuhar was a major Tamilakam trading port. From the description of the city in *Silappadikaram*, it appears that seven commodities (cloth, gold, grains, salt, oil, ploughs and jaggery) were regularly traded, and each had its own guild. City streets were designated according to the commodities, and shops were quite specialized. Flags were used to signal the location of each shop and the goods traded in that shop. There were numerous toddy shops for the weary travellers and, as per one account, 'the flags for toddy shops were so numerous that the sunlight could not penetrate onto the street below.'

Among the caravan traders of Multan, evidence shows that a *hundi*—a bill of exchange drawn up in a formulaic language—was used. An English trader called Burnes wrote about how he '…could use my Indian *hundi* in Nizhny Novgorod, Astrakhan and Bukhara.' The Multani traders had a hierarchy consisting of a general market broker (*dalal*), grain market broker (*baqal*), agents (*gumastha*) and moneylenders (*saraf*). These were fairly sophisticated commercial systems for the times.

India has held together as a state through village, caste and family rather than through central political power, as is the case with China. For good or bad, this is still evident in modern Indian politics, as well as in social policies and practises. Evolving trading practises also relied on this hierarchy of village, caste and family, and arguably, this has carried over into modern corporations as well!

The Marwari ability to adapt to situations and their flexibility of mind are important factors in their extraordinary success. The Marwari concept of the *basa* was originally to provide a cooperative lodging for fellow migrants from Rajasthan. However, these *basa*s evolved into informal training schools and networks for like-minded businessmen. The Marwaris have also used their connections for business through *gomastha*s (agents) in distant areas.

For the Multani firm, the family was at the centre, and at the heart of the family was their reputation. Without a good reputation, it would be impossible for the firm to thrive in business. Shared values in this area were essential for the survival of the firm. Over many years, apprentices were trained in critical areas like accounting, the use and rules of *hundis*, the procedures to determine interest rates and the legal systems used to sort out differences. To use the language of the modern MBA, apprentices were trained in business finance, pricing and business law. This training was considered by the Multani traders to be critical to the firm's success (human resources).

The management development and succession planning system of the Chettiars of Tamil Nadu is also a very interesting and intricate one. When a boy in a family turned eleven years old, he was inducted into the business as an assistant (*podiyan*). He worked for a decade as a *podiyan* and then became a deputy (*aduthavan*) for another ten years. In the third decade of his career, he became a shareholder (*pangali*), and at age forty-one, he was groomed to be chief (*muthalali*). This system is brilliant and can stand alongside any modern management development system.

Trade and entrepreneurship have flourished in specific communities, usually on the coasts of the country. Attitudes, practises, systems, shared values and culture have evolved in myriad ways, and these have been captured within business families. Trade is the ancestor of business, and business of scale gave birth to management as a profession. There is, therefore, an evolutionary nexus between trading, business and management.

MY EXPERIENCES AND LESSONS

I will close this final chapter with ruminations—gathered from my professional experiences—on why I am so optimistic about the role of business as a force for good in society and the nation, and on the satisfactions young people can derive from a responsible career in business and enterprise.

Looking out towards other countries—I have spent some time trying to understand how America went from being poor and struggling to great. It is, like India, a multicultural entrepôt society, democratic and libertarian. I reckon America went through three broad phases. The first phase was from Jefferson to Lincoln, a period of about ninety years. The newly independent republic was learning to deploy democratic politics and institutions, and was largely fueled by immigration, slaves and westward expansion. An Indian reader of *Team of Rivals* (2005) by historian Doris Kearns Goodwin could well get the impression that the USA was no different from the modern-day Indian heartland: Pennsylvania and Illinois could easily stand in for Bihar or Karnataka! After Lincoln dealt with the divisive issues of slavery, for a period of sixty years from Lincoln to Teddy Roosevelt, there was a period of unbridled capitalism—the era of the mafia, the great robber barons and the Californian gold rush. The century from Teddy Roosevelt to modern times can be considered as the third phase, when the state learnt to control business for the larger good through laws, democracy and justice systems. All of this has taken two-and-a-half centuries. By contrast, India can and will achieve similar progress in perhaps half the time—say 125 years. India is halfway through currently, and the best is yet to come—that is my humble view.

Throughout my work experiences, I have watched with fascination how old, inefficient jobs gave way to new, more efficient jobs. When I joined HUL in 1967, there were six factories in large cities. Over the years, every one of these factories has given way to factories in mofussil and backward areas. The thrust of HUL's industrialization into areas like Etah, Orai, Sumerpur, Jammu and Pondicherry brought with it new jobs, new skills, new employees and hope for young aspirants in a developing society. The thrust of Tata in places like Dewas, Sanand, Mundra and Kalinganagar was enterprise-led economic development at its best. It was a great pity that the Tata effort to manufacture cars in Singur met with the fate that it did, but you win some and lose some. The same holds true for the Tata effort to set up an airline with Singapore Airlines, long before the advent of other private sector airlines.

Distribution and logistics is another area that has created efficiency and jobs. The HUL thrust to relentlessly expand consumption of its products in rural areas, the jobs that such a thrust created and the prosperity that it enabled are all records of achievements towards the social good, while expanding the company's operations. Likewise, the Tata thrust into agricultural inputs to improve the yields of the Indian farmers brought a close, touch-and-feel experience for the consumers of the future. Consumer-centricity is not just an MBA phrase—a professional experiences it by walking through dusty bazaars, touching sweaty shoulders and talking to India's aspirational consumers.

In Tata, I learnt about the hope that Lakmé brought to Indian women by providing them affordable cosmetics at a time when a newly independent India thought it inappropriate to keep aside scarce foreign exchange for import of cosmetics. Lakmé is a lovely story in the Tata stable. I was personally happy that when Tata decided to exit Lakmé, the business was sold to a highly consumer-oriented company like HUL, where Lakmé has miraculously grown and prospered.

I began my career in what would today be called IT—information technology. In those days, fifty years ago, it was termed as Electronic Data Processing. After five years of IBM and ICL machines, accompanied by Autocoder and Fortran programming, I moved on to marketing and an operational career at HUL. Coming to Tata gave me a vantage point to observe how the company nurtured and persisted with IT to eventually take the jewel company of the group, Tata Consultancy Services, to global recognition—creating jobs and pioneering a whole industry worth $150 billion, estimated to employ four million young aspiring Indians.

Through these experiences and observations, how could I not feel pangs of elation that my career in business has been so elevating and worthwhile? I may be pardoned for looking back at the efforts of my many colleagues, and myself in my own small way, as lives worth living.

Societies and nations need the engines of powerful business and enterprise to create jobs, economic growth and hope for aspirants.

Acknowledgements

As the title of this book suggests, its content is a real doodle. Over the years, I have tried to express my thoughts in articles, keynote speeches and essays. Some of them were written from a transactional level balcony, while others were from a corporate or holistic level. These balconies are the natural resting places for upwardly mobile managers and leaders as they wind their way up the narrowing staircase of their personal development, gradually and thoughtfully. Such notes and writings hold a special meaning for the lonely pilgrim on the climb, because they were relevant to him or her at a certain point in time; they helped the leader view events and people in his or her set of stakeholders from different vantage points.

Therefore, like everyone who has been writing and doodling through their life and career experiences, I too have collected my contributions. It is to the credit of Kapish Mehra and Yamini Chowdhury of Rupa that they felt that the contents could provide the basis for a valuable book. For their reader insight and instinct, they need to be recognized. Much against my protests, Kapish and Yamini nudged me to put the documents together for their critical review. And then they saw what I could not see.

I must give them the credit for proposing how the writings should be restructured and rewritten to provide today's reader with a fresh and potentially valuable narrative. It has been incredibly tough work. As architects and builders are aware, it is easier to build monuments on fresh and clean ground than to refurbish old monuments. So it is with a writer. In undertaking this task, I was greatly helped by the indefatigable efforts of Yamini. She was quick, sharp and forgiving in her relentless approach, even as I struggled with some of the parts. Thank you, Yamini.

I should also mention Sourya Majumder, who went through my draft with great skill and precision, to the advantage of the book.

I must also acknowledge the support of the publications and forums that I used for the initial deployment of ideas. They have given me a platform to air the ideas and thoughts which have gone into putting this book together.

Business Standard had carried a version of the first chapter, which contains the staged conversation among the first four chairmen of Tata. The chapter on the Et Tu Movement (fifth) also owes its origins to my columns in the paper. Thank you, *Business Standard*.

The essay on my experiences as Chairman, Tata Group Innovation Forum, owes a lot to the professional colleagueship, comradeship and friendship that I developed with Ravi Arora of Tata Sons. We worked together professionally, and his assistance and painstaking writing on our experiences has contributed to the second chapter on innovation. Thanks, Ravi. He toiled to put the facts together—any failings in writing it up are all mine.

The third chapter on trusteeship comes out of the thoughts shared on Gandhi Jayanti day at a seminar at IIM Bangalore. That experience of connecting Gandhiji's teachings with modern management challenges was stimulating.

The fourth chapter was initially conceived for Brookings India for a book, *India Transformed*, published by Penguin India. I must acknowledge that my efforts to reconstruct the firm-level efforts of two great corporations—Hindustan Lever and Tata Sons—when liberalization unfolded in India, was due to the prodding of that book's editor, Rakesh Mohan. The drafts of the article were reviewed by both Susim Datta and Ratan Tata, and that helped me to get over the inevitable memory and judgement lapses that most writers suffer from.

The sixth chapter about making 'Little India' shine was initially researched by me for an event in Forum of Free Enterprise. Over the years, the prosperity and advancement of Bharat, as compared to India, has assumed greater significance, and it was meaningful to update and review my initial thoughts on the subject.

The seventh chapter about farming and agriculture was born out of a pained response to the continued indifference of policymakers to the plight of farmers. India had tried all sorts of things—could she now do something totally different? At the time I started to write about it, I was chairing an agricultural inputs company, Rallis India. The pains and inequities suffered by farmers haunted me from agricultural season to season. That continues, to my great regret.

The eighth chapter originated in a paper I wrote for the Forum of Free Enterprise charting the next fifteen years, from 2010 to 2025. I made certain assertions, and this book has given me an opportunity to review how those assertions appear now that we are halfway through. As always, some were right, but others were not!

The ninth chapter is derived from a memorial speech that I made at Bhubaneshwar. While I greatly appreciate the sagacity and foresight of our higher judiciary, I do worry a lot that the common citizen is not able to resolve judicial disputes speedily.

The tenth chapter is a current doodle. Often I have been asked by youngsters whether a business career can be satisfying, because they assume that the activities of enterprise and business are not nation and society oriented. I believe that this view is far from being true, so I have narrated my own experiences on how enterprise can be a career that also adds value socially and economically.

All in all, I have put in the effort and owe thanks to many others, but the reader is the one and only arbiter. I hope the reader finds this book to be a useful read. I am always open to reader feedback at rgopal@themindworks.me.

R. Gopalakrishnan,
Mumbai, 21 May 2019

Index

About Schmidt, 77
Agricultural policy, 111–12
Agricultural productivity, xv–xvi
Agricultural Technical Training Institutes (ATIs), 115
Agriculture Produce Market Committee (APMC) Act, 116
Agriculture Technology Training Institutes (ATTIs), 118
Alagh, Y.K., 113
American International Group (AIG), 81–82
Amichand, Motichund, 172
Andrew Carnegie Trust, 35
Angus, Mike, 79
Arora, Ravi, 11
Associated Cement Company (ACC), 61
Atomic Energy Commission, 36
Authoritativeness and leadership, 10
Axis Bank, 73
Aylwin, Patricio, 139

Badgaiyan, Ravindra, 133
Baldrige model, 62
Barnevik, Percy, 73
Barrett, Craig, 80
Bengal Famine, 135

Bhagavata Purana, 38
Bharat Financial Inclusion Limited, 159
Bharti Telecom, 57, 80, 149
Bhushan, Prashant, 133
Big Business and Entrepreneurship, 70
Bima Yojana, 118
Biocon, 57
Birkinshaw, Julian, 17, 21
Board of Control for Cricket in India (BCCI), 133
Bofors, 125, 138
Bombay Chamber, 106
Bose, Suraiya Hasan, 166
Boston Consulting Group (BCG), 143, 155
Bowen McCoy, 30
Brand Equity and Business Promotion (BEBP) Agreement, 66
Brand India, 65
British Famine Inquiry Commission, 135
'Broken windows', accountability for, 132–34
Brooke Bond, 45, 58–60
Bumper earnings, 4
Burnes, 181

Business management, 174, 178

Capitaline Database, 70
Capitalism, 29, 38
    constitutional liberalism and, 149
    crony capitalism, 65, 69
    role of, 100
    unbridled, 184
    venture capitalism, 156
Catholic-Protestant divide, 169
Central Bureau of Investigation
    (CBI), 124–26
Centralization vs. decentralization, 98
Champy, James, 76
Chandrasekaran, N., 86
Chesbrough, Henry, 24
Chettiars, planning system of, 182
Chidambaram, P., 48
Christensen, Clayton, 16, 20
Clean-up job, 82–87
Clive, Robert, 94
Coal mines, 138
'Coffingate'. *See* Kargil coffin scam
Cohen, Roger, 139
Collaborative innovation, 22–24
Colloidal India, encounters with, 171–74
Colloidal society, 168–71
Colonialism, legacies of, 147
Commonwealth Games scam, 138
Companies Act, 55, 117
Constitution of India, 134
    amended in, 1993, 98
Constitutional democracy, threat to, 134–35
Consumer-centricity, 185
Controller of capital issues, 57
Corporate governance, 57, 86
Corporate leadership, balcony of, viii–ix, xi
'Corporate Plan', 51
Corporate Social Responsibility
    (CSR), 177
Corrupt institutions, pain of, 124–26

Culture and values of Tata, 2

Dairy and poultry feeds, xv
Dairy ice cream, 58
Darbari Seth, 5, 8
Datta, Susim, 46–47, 77
Daulatram, Jairamdas, 110
De Faria, Rogeiro, 172
Decentralization
    enterprise and, xv, 89
    challenge of, 105–8
    impediment in, 107
Deming Prize, 63, 155
Democracy, 100, 120, 134, 135–36, 138, 140–41, 149, 184
Demographic dividend, 148
Desai, Xerxes, 86
Dey, Atanu, 159
Dharamsi Mills. *See* Svadeshi Mills
Digital India, 109
Divestment approach, 55
Djokovic, Novak, 74
Doom Dooma Assam, 59
Durant, Will, 144

Early Indians, 165
'Ease of doing business', 140
Economic crisis of 2008, 143
Economic growth, xv, xvii, 91–92, 145, 147, 161, 186
Economic reforms of 1991, 14
Electronic Data Processing, 186
Enterprising Indians, 93–95
Entrepreneurial behaviour, 155
Entrepreneurial energy, 175
Entrepreneurial mindset, 151–52
Entrepreneurial tradition, 179–83
Entrepreneurship, 68, 82, 95, 101, 104, 128, 151–53, 156, 159, 161, 163, 174, 176, 178, 183
Escorts, 149
Essel Propack, 157
#EtTu Movement, 72–75

Farmer producers organisations
   (FPOs), 115
Farming issue, 113–16
Fawad, 132
Federer, Roger, 74
Financial Times, 75
Flannery, John, 75, 83
Ford Foundation, 35
Foreign Direct Investment
   Confidence Index, 141
Foreign exchange, 45, 48, 52, 63, 69,
   145, 185
Foreign Exchange Regulation Act
   (FERA), 45, 47–48
Forum of Free Enterprise, 91
Frameworks, idea of conceptual, 111

Gadi Bero, 173
Gandhi, Indira, 146–47
Gandhi, Mahatma, 139
Ganguly, Ashok, 47, 77
Gapper, John, 75
Genetically Modified Organisms
   (GMO), 117
George, Bill, 78
Ghemawat, Pankaj, 65
Ghoshal, Sumantra, 48
Girhotra, Ruchika, molestation of, 124
GoAir, 80
Goods and Services Tax (GST), 116
Goodwin, Doris Kearns, 184
Governance system, 85
'Government-less civilization', xvi,
   96–98
Grand Deming Prize, 63
Greenberg, Hank, 81
Griggs, James, 91
Gross Domestic Product (GDP), viii,
   88–89, 116, 146, 148
Grove, Andy, 80
Growth spiral, 152–56
Guangdong, 44
Gujarat riots of 2002, 149
Gulf War, 45

Gupta, Rajat, 137
Gurugram, transformation of, 154

Harris, Frank, 1
Hawkins, William, 93
Heenan, David, 78
Helpless problem-solvers, pain of
   watching, 126–28
Hero MotoCorp, 157
The Hero's Farewell, 82
High Yield Variety (HYV), 117
'Hindu rate of growth', 142
Hindustan Unilever (HUL), viii,
   45–51, 54–60, 68–70, 88, 147,
   165, 176, 184–86
   company's market capitalization,
     60
   detergent division, 50
   enterprise-led economic
     development, 185
   industrialization thrust, 184–85
   integration, 55
   mergers and acquisitions, 57–60
Hitler, Adolf, 174
HLL. See Hindustan Unilever
   (HUL)
Holistic leadership, balcony of x–xii
Hundi (bill of exchange), 181
Hussaini Brahmins, 171

The Idea of Justice, 130
Immelt, Jeff, 83
Imperial Bank of India, 4
Implement Ideas, 20
Import-export trade, 148
'Incredible India@60', 88
Indebtedness, 143
'India Shining', 88
Indian Business and Nationalist Politics,
   xiii, 70
Indian Council of Agricultural
   Research (ICAR), 118
Indian Space Research Organisation
   (ISRO), 19

Indulekha (Ayurvedic hair oil), 58
Indus Valley civilization, 165
Industrial licenses, 49
Infosys, 57, 73, 149
Inglis, Mark, 32
Injustice
　feelings of, 128–29
　grounds of, 130
　pain of, 123–24
Innocentive, 24
InnoCluster, 23–24
InnoCompass. *See* Implement Ideas
InnoMeter, 21, 26–27
'InnoMultiplier', 20
Innovation ecosystem, 15–22
　demystifying innovation, 16–18
　encouraging innovation, 18–20
　measuring innovation, 21–22
InnoVista, 18, 26
'Insaniyat', xvi
'Institutional integrity', 121
Insurance Regulatory and
　Development Authority
　(IDRA), 45
Intel, 80, 158
Intellectual Property Rights (IPR), 23
International Centre for
　Entrepreneurship and Career
　Development (ICECD), 103
Iqbal, Allama Mohammed, 168, 170
IT-enabled services (ITeS) industry, 104
Iyengar Brahmins, 167

J.N. Tata Endowment Trust, 36
Janata Dal, 124
Jeejebhoy, Jamsetjee, 172
Jessica Lal, 123
Joblessness, 143
John F. Welch Technology Center
　(JFWTC), 159
Joint Stock Company, 30
Joseph, Tony, 165
JRD Quality Value Award, 63

Judiciary, corruption in, 126

Kahneman, Daniel, 143
Kalanick, Travis, 83
Kargil coffin scam, 125
Kasab, Ajmal, 134
Kasturirangan, K., 19
Katju, Markandey, 92, 126, 129
Kearney, A.T., 141, 155
Kerkar, Ajit, 5, 8, 51
Ketan Parekh scam, 131
Khadi Village Industries Corporation
　(KVIC), 104
Khan, Liaquat Ali, 8, 36
Khan, Mahira, 132
Khosla, Vinod, 159
Khosrowshahi, Dara, 83
Kidwai, Rafi Ahmed, 110
Kissan, 59
Kohli, Faqir Chand, 9
Krishna, Raj, 142

Lafley, A.G., 79
Lakmé, 185–86
Law Commission, 127–28
Leader's privilege, 37–38
Leadership moments, vii
*Leaving on Top: Graceful Exits for
　Leaders*, 78
Leverhulme Trust, 35
LGBT issue, 139
Liberalism, 139
　constitutional liberalism, 149
Liberalization, xiii, xiv, 44
　ceiling relaxation, 56
　'children of liberalization', 45–47, 69
　derivative of, 67
　GDP growth, 88
　maelstrom of, 46
　Magic of, 52
　period after, 48
　positive stories for, 65
　winds of, 60

License permit raj, 47, 52, 55, 58
Licensing Policy Enquiry Committee, 70
Lipton, 59
'Little India', 91–93, 98–99
  change agenda, 99–100
  economic growth, 100
  study on entrepreneurship in, 100
Loan waivers, 110
Lodha Committee report, 133
Lord Krishna, 38–39

Mahabharata, 39, 77, 166
Maira, Arun, 19
Make in India, 118, 128
Malcolm Baldrige National Quality Awards (MBNQA), 62
Mallya, Vijay, 59, 123
Mandela, Nelson, 139
Mandvi merchants, 180
'Mann Deshi Udyogini', 104
Manufacturing, 156–57
Marshall Plan for rural India, 159
Marwari, flexibility of mind, 182
Mashelkar, R.A., 19
Mathai, John, 8, 36, 90
Mathur, A.K., 92
McClelland, David, 95, 101, 151
McCoy, 31–32
McKinsey, 53, 56, 155
Mehta, Bezonji, 8
Menon, V.P., 97
Merchant charity, 177
Merchants of Poompuhar, 179
Mergers and acquisitions (M&A), 58
Meritocracy, principles of, 56
Metcalfe, Charles, 96
Microfinance, 159–60
Milkfoods, 59
Minimum support price (MSP), 92, 110
  revamping, 116
Modi Rubber, 149
Modi, Lalit, 123

Mohammad, Ghulam, 90
Monopolies and Restrictive Trade Practises Act, 1969 (MRTP), xiii, 45, 53, 61
Moolgaokar, Sumant, 9, 64
Moore, Gordon, 80
Morality and effective legal systems, 138–40
Morgan Stanley, 30
Moser-Baer, 157
Mountaineer's dilemma, 30–33
Muhammad, Ghulam, 36
Muhammad, Malik Ghulam, 8
Multani traders, 181–82
Mumbai terror attacks, 134
Munshi, K.M., 110
Muscle power and caste, 107
Muziris, 180

Narasimham, M., 147
Nariman, Fali, 129
National Agricultural Mission, 115
National Agricultural Policy (NAP), 112, 112
National Bank for Agricultural and Rural Development (NABARD), 114, 115, 117
National Commission for Enterprises in the Unorganized Sector (NCEUS), 92
National Commission on Farmers, 112
National Institute of Public Finance and Policy (NIFPP), 106
National Judicial Appointments Commission (NJAC), 121
National Sample Survey Office (NSSO), 101
NDA governments, 132
Nehru, Jawaharlal, 8, 93, 145
New India Assurance Company, 6
New locomotives, 142–44
The New York Times, 137, 139
Nicholson, Jack, 77

NineSigma, 24
Nirbhaya case, 130, 136
Nirma, 47
Nirvana of business, 40–41
Nohria, Nitin, 76
Non-performing assets (NPAs), 82
Non-Tata way of solving problems, 61–63

'Open innovation', 24–25
  potential for, 26
Opium trade, 172
Otellini, Paul, 80
Overseas acquisitions, 66

Palkhivala, Nani, 9, 36, 90
Panama leaks, 138
Parliament of Religions. See Vivekananda, Swami
Patanjali, 46–47, 68. See also Ramdev, Baba
Patel, Vallabhbhai, 97
Patent applications in India, 158
Patnulkarar (Saurashtrian Tamils), 173
Paulo Coelho blog, 70
Peterson, John, 7
Planning Commission, 19
Police reform, 125
Polman, Paul, 78
Poompuhar, 179, 181
Poster boys of growth, 67–69
Procter & Gamble (P&G), ix, 24, 75, 79
Profit-making companies, 56
Public credulity, 139
Public Interest Litigation (PIL), 121
Public reasoning, 135–37
Purchasing Power Parity (PPP), 148

R&D, 22–23, 25, 58, 156–159
  budgets, 158
  cost of doing, 158
Radhakrishnan, S. 149

Rajadhyaksha, Vasant, 76
Rajagopalachari, C., xvi, 96
Rallis India, 102, 118
Ramadorai, S. 86
Ramakrishna, G.V., 57
Ramdev, Baba, 68
Rao, P.V. Narasimha, 48
Rashtriya Janata Dal (RJD), 124
Rathore, S.P.S. 124
Reich, Robert, 100
Religious diversity, 149
Resolution of disputes, 102, 122
Rhodes, David, 143
Right to Education (RTE), 134
Right to Information (RTI), 134
RK Hazari Report on the Corporate Private Sector, 70
Rockefeller, John D., 33–35
Rodrik, Dani, 146
Rogay, Mohamad Ali, 172
Roosevelt, Teddy, 184
Rural employment, 142
Rural Infrastructure Services for Commons (RISC), 159
Rural MBA, 101–3
Rural non-agricultural employment (RNAE), 142
Rural Non-Farm Services (RNFS), 101

Salem Advocates Bar Association case, 127
Salman Khan hit-and-run case, 123
Sanjeeva Reddy, Neelam, 110
Santhanam, K., 98
'Sarthak Krishi Yojana', 110, 114–16
  institutions of governance, 115
  policy for farming, 115
  risk institutions and financing, 114–15
  skilling, 115
  technology incubation, 114
Scalable experiences, challenge of, 104–5

Schmidt, Warren, 77
Securities and Exchange Board of India (SEBI), 57, 131
Sen, Amartya, 130, 136, 144
Sequential Recycling and Qualitative Research, 51
'Servant leadership', 33–35
Sexual harassment, prevention of, 121
Shahabuddin, Mohammad, 124
SHARE Microfin, 159
Sharp, David, 32
Shastri, Lal Bahadur, 109
Shroff, A.D., 9, 90–91, 108
Siddis of Karnataka, 171
Simulated test markets, 51
Singapore Airlines, 65
Singh, Manmohan, 48
Sinha, Chetna Gala, 104
Skill India, 109
Small Industry Extension Training Institute (SIETI), 95
Social harmony, 150, 167
Social infrastructure, government focus, 150–51
Sonnenfeld, Jeffrey, 82
Soumya, rape and murder case, 129
Spanish Inquisition, 169
Spic, 149
Sriperumbudur corridor, entrepreneurial drive, 154
Start-up India, 109
Start-ups promise, 69
'State of Innovation', 21
State-of-the-art technology, 52
Stelter, Daniel, 143
Stepan Chemicals, 47
'Strong' laws, delusions about, 130–32
Subramaniam, Chidambaram, 110
Subramanian, Arvind, 146–47
Subramanian, C., 112
Superstar CEO, 38–40
Supply chain management, 179

Svadeshi Mills, 3
'Swachh Insaaf' initiative, 140
Syngenta India, 118

Taj Mahal hotel, 5
Talwar, Aarushi, murder case, 123
Tamil Brahmin, 166, 173
Tamilakam traders, 179
Tandon, Prakash, 76
Taobao.com, 118
Tata Airlines, 7
Tata BP Solar, 103–4
Tata Business Excellence Model (TBEM), 62–63, 65
Tata Chemicals, 39, 42, 58, 66–67
Tata Chemicals Rural Development Society (TCRDS), 102–3
Tata Code of Conduct, 65
Tata Construction, 6
Tata Consultancy Services (TCS), 42, 56–57, 61, 64–65, 86, 186
    cash flows, 64
    export revenues, 64
    initial public offering (IPO), 64–65
Tata Electro-Chemicals, 6
Tata Group Innovation Forum (TGIF), xiv, 11–13, 15–16, 18–19, 21, 24–28, 66
Tata Industrial Bank, 6
Tata Infotech, 61
Tata Innovation Day, 18
Tata InnoVista Awards, 20, 66
Tata Management Training Centre (TMTC), 17–18, 62
Tata Motors, 42, 52, 64, 66
Tata Nano, 64
Tata Oil Mills Company (TOMCO), 5–6, 54–58
Tata Power, 42, 61
Tata Quality Management Services (TQMS), 16
Tata Sons, 1, 7, 9, 11–13, 19, 42, 46, 51, 53–54, 61, 64, 86, 90

Tata Steel, 42, 52, 61, 63, 66, 155, 157
Tata Textiles, 5
Tata Vyavasai Kendra, 103
'Tata White Elephant', 5
Tata, J.R.D., 1, 13, 36, 51, 61, 64
Tata, Jamsetji, 1, 10, 13, 35
Tata, Ratan, 14, 46, 51, 53–55, 61–64
Tea Estates India, 59
Team of Rivals, 184
Tertiary employment, multiplier effect, 154
Tetley, acquisition of, 66
Texas Instruments, 156, 158
Thomas, T., 47, 77
Thong Long Huan Niao, 44
The Times of India, 136
Titan, 86
Total Productivity Maintenance (TPM), 58
TPM Excellence Award, 155
Transactional leadership, balcony of viii, xi
Transformation agenda, 55–56
Trusteeship, 29
   commitment towards, 35–37
2G scam, 138

Tyndall effect, 169

Uber, 83
UPA government, 132, 149
'Usual' Monday morning meeting, 51

Vaidya, Sitaram Khanderao, 8
Vajpayee government, 112
Venture investment, 156
Vishakha guidelines, 121
Vivekananda, Swami, 33–35
Vodafone tax dispute, 121

Wagoner, Richard, 73
The Wall Street Journal, 82
Walls Frozen Desserts, 58
Welch, Jack, 73, 75, 83
'Welding' mechanisms, 54
Wipro, 149
World Bank, 93
World War I, 4

Y2K boom, 64
Yadav, Ramkrishna, 68
Yadav, Ranvir Singh, 131–32
Zahura, 59